BETTER THAN HAPPY:

Connecting With Divinity
Through Conscious Thinking

JODY MOORE

faith matters

Book design by Deena Rutter
Cover photography by Lizzy Williams (Lizzyography)
Library of Congress Cataloging in Publication Data

Moore, Jody
Better Than Happy: Connecting with Divinity through
Conscious Thinking / Jody Moore
Subjects: Church of Jesus Christ of Latter-day Saints, LDS Life Coaching, Gospel Principles, Mental Health, Emotional Health, Happiness, Christian Life Coaching.

Paperback ISBN: 978-1-953677-07-5
Hard cover ISBN: 978-1-953677-08-2
Ebook ISBN: 978-1-953677-09-9
Audiobook ISBN: 978-1-953677-10-5

Library of Congress Control Number: 2021915712

PRINTED IN THE UNITED STATES OF AMERICA
The paper used in this publication meets the minimum requirements of the American National Standard for Information Sciences—Permanence of Paper for Printed Library Materials, ANSI Z39.48–1992
Faith Matters Publications advocates the responsible use of our natural resources. The text paper of this book is made from 30% post-consumer waste.

Acknowledgments

This book would not be possible without the patience and guidance of many people. Thank you to Faith Matters for being brave and believing in me, to Celia Barnes for repeatedly telling me the truth even when it was hard to hear, and to Deena Rutter for always making everything look beautiful.

I wouldn't be the coach, creator, or woman I am today without the work of my mentor Brooke Castillo; and I never would have found her without the guidance of my friend Kris Plachy. Thank you for being the kind of women who are not afraid to stir the pot in the name of inviting more love into the world.

Finally, a huge thank you to my team for doing all of the things I'm not good at so that I can do what I love, and to my family for making so many sacrifices in the name of my dreams and goals. I love you so.

Contents

INTRODUCTION

On a warm spring day in May 2014, I walked into a small hotel conference room to begin life coach training. I was excited to be there. In my previous corporate job as a leadership coach, I had witnessed the power of coaching, and I was eager to go on a deep dive and learn more about it. I knew this training would be fascinating and that I would enjoy the experience. But I didn't expect the level of personal transformation I would have as a result.

By the last day of coach training, I was not the person I had been on the first day, and that's not an exaggeration. I had learned things that I could not dismiss as insignificant. I saw the world, and myself, differently. On a deep level, I understood how much power I had in my own life experience, how to more often be the person I was striving to be, and how to love myself when I fell short. I had concrete tools for navigating life's challenges. I was filled with love for everyone. This new perspective has continued to serve me ever since, and as I've coached thousands of individuals, I have seen, over and over again, others adopt this perspective.

As I've observed the power of the concepts contained in this book working in people's lives, I've seen marriages that seemed hopeless become fun again. I've watched people who were full of self-doubt shift to empowerment and pursue amazing goals. I've seen depressed and anxious people learn to navigate their emotions and find joy. I've seen indecisive people learn to make decisions with confidence. I've witnessed relationships with difficult people become peaceful and easy. I've watched perfectionists and people-pleasers become authentic and connected. I've seen people who haven't been successful in the way they wanted to be succeed beyond their expectations. I've even seen the most negative of us become a force of positivity and light.

If you choose to truly examine yourself in the way I will guide you to do throughout this book, the transformations that I and so many of my clients have experienced can also happen for you, my friend.

Yes, you.

I am sure.

No matter how long you've been feeling stuck, how serious your problem is, or how unrealistic your goals may seem, the tools I will offer you can change everything.

The concepts I teach are derived from what scientists and researchers have discovered about how the human brain works. They are rooted in the fields of psychology and neurology and are distilled into applicable tools that average, highly functioning humans can use to become mentally and emotionally stronger while handling life's challenges and achieving their goals. And as a member of The Church of Jesus Christ of Latter-day Saints, I see how these principles are parallel with the gospel of Jesus Christ as taught in the scriptures and by our prophets and apostles. I rarely hear a conference talk without noticing threads of these principles woven throughout. When I read the scriptures through this lens, I find powerful insights around the doctrine as a result. I will offer these insights to you, and my hope is that you will take them and discover how they fit into your life and your values and come to your own conclusions.

Allow me to begin by explaining what I mean by *conscious thinking*. Most people believe, and I used to believe, that in order to create the lives we want, we need to get busy doing something. Many of us are action takers: when a problem arises or we want to accomplish a goal, we *do* something to try to fix the problem or achieve the goal.

Hard work. Hustle. Action.

Often when we are trying to solve a problem, we ask people, "What should I do?" And we love it when people ask us the same question because we have a lot of opinions about what other people should do. We offer strategies to try, books to read, food to eat, exercises to do, and even words to say. We are especially eager to share our advice if it's an area we've been successful with ourselves. "Here's what I did," we say, believing that what worked for us should work for pretty much anyone else. Now, I'm not saying that asking for and offering advice like this is harmful, and I am all for taking action to create the life you want. However, what we truly need is not advice about what to do—we need advice about how to think.

When we think in a useful way about our problems, ourselves, or our challenges, then we come to know what to do. What *we* should do. We discover the best possible action to take given our circumstances, our preferences, our strengths, and our limitations. We know all of these things better than anyone outside of us does. When we think clearly, in a conscious manner, we open ourselves up to receive personal revelation about what we should do—not necessarily what someone else did or thinks we should do.

For example, I can tell you what I think you should say to your troubled daughter. But I'm not you, so my words aren't as authentic as your words would be, and I don't know your daughter as well as you do. You truly know better than I do what to say to her. The reason you think you don't know is because of your thoughts: "I don't know what to say. I want to say the right thing. I don't want to upset her." These are all thoughts. They sound like reasonable thoughts, but if they block you from knowing what to say, then they might not be serving you. Thinking consciously means taking a look at your thoughts and then deliberately choosing what you want to think, instead of settling for the default thoughts your brain offers.

"I will know what to say when the time comes. The Spirit will guide me. There is no 'right' thing to say. I love my daughter enough to be honest with her even if she doesn't want to hear it." These thoughts, more than the previous ones, will probably help you show up as the mother you want to be. These thoughts open you up to receive answers from the Spirit. Believing these thoughts will take you ten times further toward the outcome you would like than my opinion of what you should say. Understanding this concept and then doing the work to think *deliberately* is what I call *conscious thinking*.

In the coming chapters, I'm going to offer you more tools and examples to aid in your ability to think consciously. Sometimes I will refer to this process as "doing thought-work." If you choose to try these tools, you can learn how to think deliberately instead of simply believing your default thoughts, and as a result, you will experience the miraculous transformation within you and in your life.

You're going to read many examples of the power of consciously choosing your thoughts, and I hope that the examples will aid in providing you a concrete understanding of how to utilize this work in your life. I'm going to share examples from my own life, from the scriptures, and from some of my clients (whose names have been changed to protect their privacy). But I also want to connect the dots between the principles of the gospel of Jesus Christ and the tools I use in my work as a coach to help my clients with their thoughts.

Consciously choosing your thoughts alone is powerful. It really is. But for me, this power is magnified tenfold when combined with the true doctrine of the restored Church. The gospel is the tool by which I find I can search, ponder, and pray, which allows me to receive personal revelation and answers to prayers. The knowledge I have gained about human behavior through my work as a life coach has also helped me catch a tiny glimpse of some of the incredible wisdom and love behind the Lord's plan for us. This insight has helped me see that the commandments I've been taught and try to follow make perfect sense, and it has helped me know how to pick myself up and get back on track when I fail to be the person I want to be.

Learning to think consciously has helped me understand how to truly live from the belief that we have nothing to fear thanks to Jesus Christ's Atonement. Conscious thinking has given me the tools to develop faith and peace in my heart and bones instead of just understanding intellectually that faith and peace are available in this life. For me, these tools have connected the dots of why and how in regard to many of the gospel principles I'd been striving to live my entire life. As I share this insight with you, my hope is that we can all gain a deeper awareness of ourselves mentally, emotionally, and spiritually.

Each chapter of this book is centered around a gospel principle so that, at any time, you can take a deep dive into a specific topic you want to explore. However, I recommend that the first time you read the book you read each chapter in order because some concepts will build upon tools taught in previous chapters.

I am fascinated with the human mind, and I believe that loving Heavenly Parents know us and our tendencies well enough to give us commandments that will ultimately lead to our greatest joy and success in this life and the next. Conscious thinking is one tool that may help you live what you believe, as it has helped me and others do. And if the fruits of this work provide you with the sweetness they have provided for us, then perhaps it is of God, for all that is good is of God.[1] Are you ready? Come with me.

———————

1. Moroni 7:12.

For we labor diligently to write, to persuade our children, and also our brethren, to believe in Christ, and to be reconciled to God; for we know that it is by grace that we are saved, after all we can do.

2 Nephi 25:23

01. GRACE

Two Parts

I was walking around T.J.Maxx with a shopping cart and no particular objective beyond avoiding the more productive things I should have been doing on a Thursday afternoon when my phone buzzed in my back pocket. *Who would be calling me?* I thought. Nobody calls. We send text messages now. And if we *are* going to call someone, we have to text first to ask the person if she is able to talk, even though we all know that if she isn't able to talk she *could* just not answer. At any rate, I checked my phone and saw that it was my sister Lindsay calling.

"Hi, Linds!" I said, remembering how much I'd been looking forward to hearing from her.

Lindsay is six years younger than me and at the time lived two states away, but we've always been close. She was about twenty weeks pregnant with her second child and had gone in that day for the ultrasound that would show the baby's gender. She was probably calling to report the news, which, by the way, is a valid reason for an unscheduled, unvetted phone call to your sister.

"So . . . pink or blue?"

"Um, yeah, about that . . ." she said in a more nervous tone than I was expecting.

"What? What is it? Is everything OK?" I asked.

"Well, yes. I mean it will be. It's twins," she said. She sounded overwhelmed.

"*What*? Twins? They didn't know until *now* that you're having *twins*?"

"Nope," she laughed.

She explained that her doctor was "old school" and hadn't picked up on this detail of her pregnancy and that they hadn't done an ultrasound until today. But she was definitely having two babies.

Two girls.

Fraternal twins.

While I thought this was the best news ever, as you might imagine Lindsay and her husband had more complicated emotions. They shifted from overwhelm to excitement to fear and back to love throughout the remainder of the pregnancy and for the first few years of raising those two sweet girls. Although two babies was a huge surprise, we are blessed to have Maddy and Katie in our family, and now it feels as though something would be awfully wrong if they hadn't come to earth together.

Today, my five-year-old nieces and their silly antics keep us all on our toes, and I'm grateful to now live just a few miles away from them. In many ways the twins couldn't be more opposite, but in other ways they are peas in a pod. We love them both equally and individually. We wouldn't celebrate the birthday of one girl and not the other. We wouldn't buy a gift for one and not get something for the other. We don't love, appreciate, or value one more than the other. Of course they are individuals, and as they get older they will probably crave more time apart, but they are both amazing, beautiful, and equally loved additions to our family. This experience will seem obvious to anyone who knows and loves twins. But as I have seen what a gift these two girls are to our family, I've come to realize that the Atonement of Christ is also a two-part gift, but it is for all of us, the children of our Heavenly Parents.

I feel deeply inadequate and unqualified to be writing about Christ's Atonement because I am still trying to understand the magnitude of this gift and how to better apply it to my life. The topic seems too important and complicated for me to tackle, especially so early on in this book, but I wish to address it here because, as members of the Church, we believe that the Atonement is the most transcendent undertaking in the ongoing history of humanity.[1] Therefore, it is absolutely central to our belief system. And the gift of Christ's Atonement contains two parts.

Twin blessings.

Like my twin nieces, these blessings are equally valuable and important. However, sometimes they are not equally understood or expressed.

The first part is the redeeming power of the Atonement. We all make mistakes, but if we choose to repent, we will be forgiven, and Christ will enter our lives and work to make us whole. Elder Dieter F. Uchtdorf said, "Christ came to save us. If we have taken a wrong course, the Atonement of Jesus Christ can give us the assurance that sin is *not* a point of no return."[2] This is the part of the Atonement I tend to think about the most, the twin that often receives more attention. But there is a second part, and it is equally important to our salvation.

In a speech given at BYU, Elder David A. Bednar said, "I suspect that you and I are much more familiar with the nature of the redeeming power of the Atonement than we are with the enabling power of the Atonement. It is one thing to know that Jesus Christ came to earth to *die* for us. That is foundational to the doctrine of Christ. But we also need to appreciate that the Lord desires, through His Atonement and by the power of the Holy Ghost, to *live* in us—not only to direct us but also to empower us."[3] This second part of the Atonement, or the twin of the redeeming power, is the enabling power, also known as grace. Elder Bednar continues, "Grace represents that divine assistance or heavenly help each of us will desperately need to qualify for the celestial kingdom. Thus the enabling power of the Atonement strengthens us to do and be good and serve beyond our own individual desire and natural capacity. In my personal scripture study I often insert the term *enabling power* whenever I encounter the word *grace*."[4]

While Christ's Atonement cannot be easily explained and should be individually applied in our lives, we do know that to access the first part—the redeeming power of the Atonement— we must repent. But how do we access the second part, or the enabling power? When we are in need of the strengthening and enabling power of grace, how do we show our submission, willingness, and desire to rely on Christ's divine gift to us? How can we allow the Atonement to "strengthen us to do and be good"? I believe that one way is to pay attention to our thoughts and feelings and then ask the Lord to help us to choose them more deliberately. Our thoughts influence us in ways we don't always recognize, and if we learn to observe and choose them carefully, we can open ourselves up to grace. Which brings me to the model.

The model is a tool created by Brooke Castillo, who is the owner and founder of The Life Coach School, where I was certified as a coach six years ago and then as a master coach a few years later.[5] The model is the foundation for all the work I do

THE MODEL

CIRCUMSTANCE
The facts.

THOUGHT
Our interpretation of the facts.

FEELING
One word.

ACTION
How we show up when fueled by that feeling.

RESULT
The experience we create for ourselves overall.

as a coach, and I want to teach it to you here at the beginning of the book because it will be necessary for understanding every other chapter. Just like the Atonement of Jesus Christ is the most critical part of God's plan for us, and without it nothing else works, the model is the foundation for all the strategies of conscious thinking that I'll be teaching you here.

That said, at times you may find yourself or others in your life wanting to argue with the validity of the model, and you can. The model is *not* like the Atonement: Christ's Atonement is a divinely orchestrated, perfect gift with a significance we can barely understand, while the model is simply a tool Brooke Castillo created to help us examine ourselves so that we can gain leverage over our thoughts, feelings, and actions.

By the end of this book, if I do my job right, you are going to see the simultaneous simplicity and complexity of the model, and you will likely recognize it as something you've heard or known before but is now simplified and organized in a useful way. Brooke created the model after many years as a student of self-help and after coaching thousands of clients she helped even before she had this tool. She based it on her combined study and observations of human behavior and on her own experiences as a student and a teacher of conscious thinking. The model has enabled me and many others to access our best selves and live our best lives by emphasizing one of the most useful and critical things we can focus on:

Our inner selves.

Who we are being on the inside more than what is happening on the outside. What thoughts and feelings are driving us rather than what outside thing is triggering us. The scriptures say, "Behold, the Lord requireth the heart and a willing mind,"[6] which is where the model helps us place our focus.

Inward.

On our hearts and minds.

In our human state, we tend to view outward things as the cause of our problems or as the potential answer to our struggles, but in truth, the cause never exists outside of us. Our problems are all created inwardly; therefore, the solutions are created inwardly as well.

Here's how it works.

The Self-Coaching Model

The model consists of the following five parts, and each part affects the one after it:

Circumstance

Thought

Feeling

Action

Result

Let's break down the model and look at each part in more detail, starting with the first.

Circumstance

Circumstances are things that happen outside of us. They are the facts of a situation. A circumstance is something that everyone would agree on or that we could prove in a court of law:

Target is located at the corner of Sprague and Evergreen.

There are seven pairs of pants, eighteen T-shirts, and one pair of underwear in my son's laundry this week.

We are moving an average of twelve miles per hour on the freeway.

Sometimes changing a circumstance is an option, but sometimes it is not. For example, if I have a job (circumstance) that I don't enjoy, I could quit that job and change the circumstance. But if I have a father (circumstance) whom I find to be challenging, I don't get to sign up for a new father. I could choose to cut my father out of my life, and that might be the right move for some people in some cases, but as you can see, things get messy, and circumstance-swapping may not always serve us in the end. In addition, the circumstance is the only part of the model that isn't in our control—at least not directly. We might try to influence our father, and perhaps we can be successful in some ways, but ultimately we can't control him, just like we can't control other circumstances because they exist outside of us. Even though we try to do it all the time.

We try to manipulate, control, or change circumstances because we give external things more power than is useful. We are constantly thinking we need to move to a different house, relocate to a new city, be closer to family, get away from family, buy a different car, lose weight, make more money, get our kids to behave, get the house in order, help our children not be upset, convince our spouse to stop being so grumpy, or be more included by the women in the ward. We think that if we can change the circumstances outside of us, then we can feel better. But the real power doesn't come from outside of us. It comes from within. It comes from our thoughts.

Thought

As we become aware of circumstances, we immediately have opinions or ideas about them, also known as *thoughts*. Thoughts are the meaning we give to circumstances.

Circumstance: Target is located at the corner of Sprague and Evergreen.

Thought: We should go to Target right now and see if there is anything we didn't know we wanted to buy.

Circumstance: There are seven pairs of pants, eighteen T-shirts, and one pair of underwear in my son's laundry this week.

Thought: It's concerning that my son changes his shirt three times a day and his underwear almost never.

Circumstance: We're moving an average of twelve miles per hour on the freeway.

Thought: This is so frustrating.

Thoughts are where things get interesting. Our ability to think in such a complex manner about the things happening outside of us is what makes us the most evolved species on the planet. It's also one reason we create so much suffering for ourselves. My cat, Oscar, was not offended when the vet said that Oscar was overweight. My cat is not capable of thinking the series of thoughts that I have when my doctor delivers the same news to me. This complex thinking we do as humans is both a gift and a trial.

Our brains are *so* busy thinking countless thoughts and trying to read people and predict events that it's no wonder most of us are exhausted. The latest research shows we have approximately 6,200 thoughts per day.[7] All of these thoughts fly through our brains very quickly and create our feelings, which is the next part of the model.

Feeling

Feelings (or emotions) are created by thoughts. Feelings are not created by anything outside of us, despite what we seem to believe. Our bodies create our feelings at the direction of our brains. It's miraculous how our Heavenly Parents created us. We think a thought, our internal organs release chemicals and hormones, and then we feel their effects as they circulate throughout our bodies. They may feel tight, hot, tense, queasy, buzzy, heavy, fast. Or they may feel light, soft, warm, full, smooth, resonant, or energizing.

> **Circumstance:** We're going an average of twelve miles per hour on the freeway.
> **Thought:** This is so frustrating.
> **Feeling:** Irritated.

We attribute our feelings to our circumstances when we say things like "I'm irritated because we're going so slow." However, if we weren't thinking "This is so frustrating," we wouldn't be feeling irritated. In fact, let's play with other options.

> **Circumstance:** We are going an average of twelve miles per hour on the freeway.
> **Thought:** It looks like by the time I get home the kids will all be in bed and I will get to miss the bedtime mania.
> **Feeling:** Relieved.

Same circumstance. Different thought. Different feeling. Elder Lynn G. Robbins taught this concept when he said:

> A cunning part of his [Satan's] strategy is to dissociate anger from agency, making us believe that we are victims of an emotion that we cannot control. We hear, "I lost my temper." Losing one's temper is an interesting choice of words that has become a widely used idiom. To "lose something" implies "not meaning to," "accidental," "involuntary," "not responsible"—careless perhaps but "not responsible."

"He made me mad." This is another phrase we hear, also implying lack of control or agency. This is a myth that must be debunked. No one makes us mad. Others don't make us angry. There is no force involved. Becoming angry is a conscious choice, a decision; therefore, we can make the choice not to become angry. *We* choose![8]

To Elder Robbins's insightful teaching, I would add that the way in which we choose anger or a different emotion is by choosing what we will think in any given circumstance. Let's look at an example from the scriptures. In the Book of Mormon we learn about Lehi, Sariah, and their family, who traveled in the wilderness for many years after the Lord told them to leave Jerusalem. The facts of their situation are the circumstances. The conditions of their journey—including weather, supplies, babies born, available food or lack thereof—are all circumstances. But these circumstances didn't create the travelers' individual experiences. Thoughts did. In 1 Nephi 17:20–21, we hear Laman describe his thoughts about the circumstances as he speaks to Nephi:

> And thou art like unto our father, led away by the foolish imaginations of his heart; yea, he hath led us out of the land of Jerusalem, and we have wandered in the wilderness for these many years; and our women have toiled, being big with child; and they have borne children in the wilderness and suffered all things, save it were death; and it would have been better that they had died before they came out of Jerusalem than to have suffered these afflictions.
>
> Behold these many years we have suffered in the wilderness, which time we might have enjoyed our possessions

and the land of our inheritance; yea, and we might have been happy.

Laman's thoughts about his experience in the wilderness created the way he felt about it. Most likely, he felt anger, resentment, frustration, overwhelm, and fear when he was thinking these thoughts. But in the same circumstance, traveling through the wilderness for many years, Nephi had a different experience. We hear Nephi's thoughts in 1 Nephi 17:2–3:

> And so great were the blessings of the Lord upon us, that while we did live upon raw meat in the wilderness, our women did give plenty of suck for their children, and were strong, yea, even like unto the men; and they began to bear their journeyings without murmurings.
>
> And thus we see that the commandments of God must be fulfilled. And if it so be that the children of men keep the commandments of God he doth nourish them, and strengthen them, and provide means whereby they can accomplish the thing which he has commanded them; wherefore, he did provide means for us while we did sojourn in the wilderness.

Same circumstances. Different thoughts. Different feelings. Most likely, Nephi felt gratitude, love, hope, joy, and happiness as a result of these thoughts.

Modern prophets and apostles have counseled us about the power of our thoughts and the importance of remembering that we create our feelings. Elder David A. Bednar said, "When we believe or say we have been offended, we usually mean we feel insulted, mistreated, snubbed, or disrespected. And certainly clumsy, embarrassing, unprincipled, and mean-spirited things do occur in our interactions with other people that would allow us to take offense. However, it ultimately is impossible for another person to offend you or to offend me. Indeed, believing that another person offended us is fundamentally false. To be offended is a *choice* we make; it is not a *condition* inflicted or imposed upon us by someone or something else."[9]

Knowing that thoughts create your feelings doesn't mean thinking happy thoughts about everything and feeling positive emotions all the time. It doesn't mean that you will always be able to have positive thoughts, even when you want to have them. We will dive into the complexities of this concept in later chapters. But having this knowledge will empower you far beyond what you might be currently experiencing, and I believe it is part of how we access the enabling power of Christ's Atonement. With His help, we can align our thinking and feeling in a way that will allow Him to guide us to take the most useful possible action, which is the next part of the model.

Action

Our feelings fuel our actions. So, as we're going about our day, the things we do, the things we don't do, and the way in which we show up in the world (our actions) are the result of the emotions (or feelings) driving us.

Young kids don't try to hide their emotions. They act on every one of them. When my four-year-old daughter, Taylor, gets frustrated with her brother, she yells, stomps her feet (surprisingly loudly for such a tiny person), and sometimes even hits him. Her feelings are obvious. Now, remember, she's not frustrated because her brother is using the TV to play Xbox and won't let her watch *My Little Pony*. She's frustrated because of her thoughts. One of her main thoughts might be "This isn't fair!" That thought triggers the emotion of frustration, which she doesn't know what to do with at such a young age, so she acts out. This display of emotion makes the action line of a child's model easy to fill in.

But adults are different. We know how to be polite and pretend to be fine when we're really having a tantrum inside.

We smile and fake it.

Or we withdraw and wonder why nobody is stepping up to take care of us.

We know how to say the right words, but the emotion behind our words matters. Most of us are not Meryl Streep or Tom Hanks. We are terrible actors. So, even though we don't display our feelings like a four-year-old does, our emotions show up in our tone or in other subtleties of our behavior. We become more or less effective at any given task depending on the thoughts and feelings fueling our actions. Let's look at our example of being in traffic on the freeway.

> **Circumstance:** We're going an average of twelve miles per hour on the freeway.
> **Thought:** This is so frustrating.
> **Feeling:** Irritated.
> **Action:** Drive with a heavy foot on the gas and brake. Ruminate about the problems this traffic is creating for me and what I wish I were doing instead of sitting in the car. Worry and stress, which escalates my negative feelings. Possibly start speeding once traffic picks up.

Now, even if you are not headed home at bedtime with small children but instead are late for an important appointment, you still have the ability to choose thoughts that will create more useful feelings and drive more useful actions as a result. Here's one possibility:

Circumstance: We're going an average of twelve miles per hour on the freeway.

Thought: I guess I'm going to be late, and that's OK.

Feeling: Calm.

Action: Think about solutions like letting people know I'm running late or covering my obligations in some other way. Decide to use the time to listen to a podcast or music or to call my sister. Drive in a more calm, responsible manner.

As you can see, each of these models is likely to create a different result, which is the final part of the model.

Result

Our result in any given circumstance is due to the thoughts we think, the feelings we feel, and the actions we take. These are the parts of the model we have control over, and they are truly the parts that create our reality. The result line of the model always connects back to the thought line in some way. Let's look at our traffic examples again.

Option 1

Circumstance: We're going an average of twelve miles per hour on the freeway.

Thought: This is so frustrating.

Feeling: Irritated.

Action: Drive with a heavy foot on the gas and brake. Ruminate about the problems this traffic is creating for me and what I wish I were doing instead of sitting in the car. Possibly start speeding once traffic picks up.

Result: I am frustrating myself and probably others. I'm having a frustrating experience while driving and am more likely to get into an accident or get a speeding ticket.

Option 2

Circumstance: We're going an average of twelve miles per hour on the freeway.

Thought: I guess I'm going to be late, and that's OK.

Feeling: Calm.

Action: Think about solutions like letting people know I'm running late or covering my obligations in some other way. Decide to use the time to listen to a podcast or music or to call my sister. Drive in a more calm, responsible manner.

Result: I'm OK. I have an OK time while driving and am more likely to get to my destination safely and be pleasant company for myself and others.

We all cause ourselves to feel bad at times, and it's tempting to blame other people or events for it. But when we make external things responsible for our own experience, we delegate the control over our results to outside things that might never change. Our brains believe that we will lose control of people or events if we let go of our negative thoughts about them—until we realize that we never had control in the first place. Thinking "I'm so frustrated that traffic is slow" doesn't make the traffic move faster. It only causes our own pain and decreases our ability to access creative solutions and strength. In other words, when we don't take responsibility for our own results, we lose access to grace.

Instead of blaming things outside of us for how we feel, we have the option to watch our thoughts, as King Benjamin recommends in the Book of Mormon. In Mosiah 4:30 he advises his people, "But this much I can tell you, that if ye do not watch yourselves, and your thoughts, and your words, and your deeds, and observe the commandments of God, and continue in the faith of what ye have heard concerning the coming of our Lord, even unto the end of your lives, ye must perish. And now, O man, remember, and perish not."

I wonder what King Benjamin meant by *perish*. To perish essentially means "to die," and every one of us is subject to death. So perhaps his meaning of *perish* is less about literal death and more about missing out on the rich experience available to us when we deliberately, consciously choose our thoughts, words, and deeds.

Watching our thoughts can be difficult, though, and sometimes we need to step back from a situation to recognize what exactly we are thinking and discover whether these thoughts are serving us. A client, Kayla, once told me that her husband, Tim, had insulted her; this was her circumstance. I pointed out that since circumstances are facts everyone would agree on, and we don't all agree on what is considered an insult, we needed to find the facts. The fact (circumstance) was that Tim said, "I really don't like this chicken you made for dinner tonight." Please note: What he said is not good or bad, kind or mean, understandable or unforgiveable until we have a thought about it. His words didn't hurt her. If he had said them in a language she didn't understand or if she hadn't heard him, she wouldn't feel hurt. She felt insulted because of her thoughts. Together Kayla and I discovered that she had all sorts of thoughts about Tim's comment:

That's so rude.

He doesn't appreciate me.

If he really loved me he would never say that.

I would never say something like that to him or anyone else (and therefore he shouldn't either).

He should keep thoughts like that to himself.

He thinks I'm a terrible cook.

He doesn't think I'm a good wife.

He thinks I'm a failure of a person.
Maybe he's right.

It's OK that Kayla was thinking these thoughts. Nothing was wrong with her. Maybe we should send Tim off to somebody who might teach him manners or, better yet, put him in charge of dinner from now on. I could get behind any of this. But sometimes attempts to control other people fail, and before we try anything like that, we want to make sure we are thinking about the situation in the most useful way possible. But please remember that as you examine your thoughts it is never useful to judge them. We have good reasons for thinking the thoughts we think—or at least our brains believe we do.

Kayla felt offended when Tim said he didn't like her dinner, but the feeling of offended did not come from his words. It came from her main thought, "That was rude." She judged him for judging her dinner and took his criticism personally; that is the reason she felt offended. If she had been in a different state of mind, she might have made Tim's comment mean something about his food preferences, his idea of what is kind or unkind, or his thoughts and feelings. His comment wasn't about her. It was about chicken. But that's not what she heard. She heard a personal attack on herself, and she made the comment mean something negative about Tim. Both of those judgments would feel terrible to any of us.

> **Circumstance:** Tim said, "I really don't like this chicken you made for dinner."
> **Thought:** That was rude.
> **Feeling:** Offended.

Kayla tried to hide what she was thinking and pretend to not be affected at dinner that night. That was the action line of her model. But she was fuming inside. She faked a smile when appropriate, but she mostly withdrew from the dinner conversation and retreated into her own head where she generated more and more thoughts about Tim and his rude behavior. She began ruminating on other times he had been rude, and now her story was shifting to "He is always so rude to me" as she filled a mental file cabinet full of evidence for this thought. She didn't hear much of what her family was saying, and she certainly didn't acknowledge Tim for the rest of the meal.

Kayla's result was that she interpreted Tim as being incredibly rude. She found lots of evidence for this painful story. She even realized (later, as I was coaching her) that in that moment she was not being the kind of mom or woman she wants to be. In fact, she was being sort of rude. I know I've helped my clients correctly piece together their model when the result is connected to the original thought. Whatever we think we will ultimately create for ourselves. Let's take a look at Kayla's complete model:

> **Circumstance:** Tim said, "I really don't like this chicken you made for dinner."
>
> **Thought:** That's so rude!
>
> **Feeling:** Offended.
>
> **Action:** Withdraw from dinner conversation and ruminate on other examples of Tim's rudeness.
>
> **Result:** I prove to myself that he is rude, and I am rude at dinner.

If Kayla wants to feel good and be her best self, then in this situation it doesn't serve her to think the thought "That's so rude." Thinking it means she has to feel offended. That's probably not the feeling she would choose if she were able to pick any feeling she wanted. Furthermore, thinking negative thoughts about Tim didn't get him to be more lovely. It resulted only in pain for Kayla, and then she became rude, and Tim could have become even more rude in response.

But do you know what is true, my friend? I get to think, feel, do, and create *any* result I want to for myself.

So does Kayla.

And so do you.

Even though we can't go back in time and relive the dinner conversation from last week, it's helpful to observe ourselves after the fact so that we gain more awareness of all the things we can control, like our thoughts, feelings, and actions. Once we have this awareness, we can train ourselves to stop trying to control things we can't control, like husbands.

And, by the way, I'm not talking about looking into a mirror and telling yourself affirmations that you don't really believe. I'm talking about thinking a new believable thought that feels better. Sometimes it's a baby step toward feeling better. Can you take a baby step in the direction that you want to go, for your own sake? Baby-step thoughts often just have a modifier before or after the original thought—for example:

That was rude, but I'm OK.

It's possible that what he said wasn't rude.

I'm believing that was rude, but maybe it wasn't.

That was rude, but he probably didn't mean it to be.

I thought that was rude, but he may not realize I think that.

Let's put one of these thoughts into a model:

Circumstance: Tim said, "I really don't like this chicken you made for dinner."

Thought: I thought that was rude, but he may not realize I think that.

Feeling: Curious.

Action: I talk to him about my thoughts and listen to what he has to say.

Result: I understand him a little bit more, and I feel heard.

Some of you may think that I'm oversimplifying the situation or that this model is great for a small problem but some things in life are more complicated and serious. My sister Natalie Clay is a coach who works with couples on improving their marriages and family dynamics, and I love the story she tells about teaching the model to a husband and wife who wanted coaching on how to deal with their rebellious teenaged daughter. Natalie wrote the model out with examples on a whiteboard. At the end of her teaching the husband said, "That's nice, Natalie. But we have a problem that your little whiteboard can't solve." If you're thinking some version of that comment, I want to recommend that you remain open and stay with me. Because there is literally *no* problem that the model can't solve. It ended up being true for Natalie and her clients, and it can be true for you as well.

The bottom line is this: Your brain is a powerful tool. It's your most valuable asset. When you spend some time observing it, you'll find that it is responsible for every single result in your life. It doesn't matter what country or family you were born into. It doesn't matter what happens or doesn't happen to you as a child or at any point in your life. In any situation, you get to choose your result, and the result will never come from the circumstance. It will come from everything that follows—from your thoughts, your feelings, and your actions. President Russell M. Nelson said, "The joy we feel has little to do with the circumstances of our lives and everything to do with the focus of our lives."[10]

For me, understanding the model and using it to become aware of myself has been life altering. While the model is simple, seeing its direct application in the world and then in your own life takes time and practice. I've been studying it for more than seven years, and I continue to gain deeper insights with more practice and experience. Expecting to use the model perfectly not only is unnecessary but will likely prevent you from making progress. So be patient and compassionate with yourself, but open your mind up to the idea that you are responsible for every emotion and every result in your life. As you do this, you will become an unstoppable force with the ability to create literally anything you want to create.

My oldest, Isaac, is a linear, logical, and you might even say serious, child. He is currently fourteen years old, but he's always been an older soul who prefers sitting with the adults at family dinner over being rowdy with the cousins in the basement.

When he was younger, his aversion to chaos and his approach to life was challenging for me. At school he was often overwhelmed at the havoc created by all those kids in one place, and he was afraid he wouldn't be able to find me at school pick-up. I reassured him he had nothing to fear, but he seemed to become more anxious the more I told him this. He wanted to stay home on evenings and weekends instead of going to the park or the movies. I didn't understand this child. I had a variety of thoughts about his behavior. I thought he was negative, ungrateful, and not choosing happiness, and I created loads of frustration for myself with these thoughts. Even worse, this sort of thinking diminished my ability to be the kind of mother I wanted to be. My model looked like this:

Circumstance: Isaac says, "I just want to stay home."

Thought: He's so grumpy all the time, and he needs to learn to be happy.

Feeling: Annoyed.

Action: I am cold to Isaac. I pout inside. I try to talk him out of feeling how he feels and lecture him regularly about happiness being a choice and one he should choose if he wants to have a good life.

Result: I notice Isaac is even more unhappy, and I'm also unhappy about his unhappiness.

This was some of the first work I did when I learned the model. By taking a look at my model, I realized that I was the one who was unhappy and grumpy. Even if Isaac was grumpy, my grumpiness was created by my own thoughts. Isaac just wants to be home during his evenings and weekends to get away from the stimulus of the world. He's an introvert. Being an extrovert myself, I couldn't understand this, and I judged him as being wrong in some way or as missing out on some important part of life. Once I realized this, I began working on a new model. It took me a while, but I did eventually get there. My new model looked like this:

Circumstance: Isaac says, "I just want to stay home."

Thought: I want Isaac to be himself even if what he wants to be is grumpy.

Feeling: Loving.

Action: I view Isaac through an entirely different lens. I see the beauty of who he is. I stop trying to talk him out of his feelings or desires. I give him space to be and find himself, even when he chooses unhappiness. I just love him as he is.

Result: I love Isaac, and I feel good about who I'm being as his mom.

Please know that I didn't just write out a model, choose a new thought, and check the box in one afternoon or one week. I failed at it for months before I was able to believe the new thought. Sometimes it takes time. That's OK. We have a lifetime—and probably eternity as well—to work on our thoughts. But I promise that as you apply the model (which I will continue to use to teach you all the other tools I'm going to offer) and petition the Lord to help you think about things in a more useful way, to see things as He sees them, you will notice that it will become difficult to identify whether the people and things outside of you are changing or if it's just you thinking differently. Most times it will just be you. This feels like magic, but it's not. It's what Christ made possible for us through the strengthening and enabling power of the Atonement, commonly called grace. My clients often describe it by saying, "Nothing has really changed and yet everything has changed."

My husband's demeanor is similar to my son's, and he is also a more compassionate and all-around better person than I am, so he never struggled to understand our son like I did. He didn't have to practice conscious thinking about Isaac's personality. A couple years ago I said to him, "Isaac has become so much more positive as he's gotten older, don't you think?" He looked at me and smiled. Then he told me the loving truth: "No, I think he's just the same as he's always been. He's always been a great kid. I think you have just become more positive about Isaac."

My hair, my kids, my money, my husband, what I ate, what I got done, what I didn't get done, my body, the dishes in the sink, the complaint that woman had about me, and whoever is the president of the United States—these are all circumstances.

They have no power over me except the power I give to them.

I am the creator of every single emotion and result that I experience.

And so are you, my friend.

I hope you see that this is good news because I assure you it is. Being the creators of our emotions and results means that instead of trying to control the world outside of us, we only have to be willing to look inward—to examine ourselves without judgment and to learn to redirect our thinking for good. Which reminds me, I have only one rule for you as you read this book:

No judging yourself.

No judging your thoughts or your models.

You can judge me if you want to. You can disagree with what I teach. But judging yourself sends all of your thoughts back into hiding and you'll lose the awareness that I hope you'll receive. It's what Satan wants you to do because he knows you will be unable to reach your divine potential if you believe you are not good enough.[11]

When you are aware of your thoughts, feelings, actions, and results, you become accountable for the experiences you have in this life. As Elder Lynn G. Robbins said, "Being 100 percent responsible is accepting yourself as the person in control of your life. If others are at fault and need to change before further progress is made, then you are at their mercy and they are in control over the positive outcomes or desired results in your life."[12]

I will share many more tools to assist you in choosing your thoughts and creating deliberate results, but for now let's take a look at one more example from the scriptures of the power that comes from focusing on our own thoughts, feelings, and actions instead of the circumstances outside of our control.

In 1 Nephi 7 we read about the time Nephi found himself bound by cords at the hands of his younger brothers Laman and Lemuel, who planned to kill him. As Nephi prayed to enlist the Lord's help, he emphasized getting help within the controllable parts of his own model. In verse 17: "But it came to pass that I prayed unto the Lord, saying: O Lord, according to my faith which is in thee [Thought: I believe you can help me. Feeling: Faith], wilt thou deliver me from the hands of my brethren [Result]; yea, even give me strength that I may burst these bands with which I am bound [Action]." Speaking of this story, Elder David A. Bednar said,

I personally do not believe the bands with which Nephi was bound just magically fell from his hands and wrists. Rather, I suspect that he was blessed with both persistence and personal strength beyond his natural capacity, that he then "in the strength of the Lord" (Mosiah 9:17) worked and twisted and tugged on the cords and ultimately and literally was enabled to break the bands.

Brothers and sisters, the implication of this episode for each of us is quite straightforward. As you and I come to understand and employ the enabling power of the Atonement in our personal lives, we will pray and seek for strength to change our circumstances rather than praying for our circumstances to be changed. We will become agents who "act" rather than objects that are "acted upon" (2 Nephi 2:14).[13]

Here's another way to describe Elder Bednar's teaching: when we understand and employ the enabling power of the Atonement, we will pray for strength to change our *results* rather than praying for our circumstances to be changed.

You don't have to control the outside world to feel however you want to feel and create any result you want to create.

What a relief.

For a long time I tried to control external things, and sometimes I felt successful, but mostly it was tough and I was exhausted. I found that looking inward and working on myself is a whole lot easier. I believe it's what the Lord wants me to do, and I believe it's possible for every one of us. And I also believe that self-reflection, self-improvement, and God's perfect knowledge of how we create results are the reasons for every gospel principle and commandment we've been given.

Let's take a closer look.

1. James E. Faust, "The Atonement: Our Greatest Hope," *Ensign*, October 2001, https://www.churchofjesuschrist.org/study/general-conference/2001/10/the-atonement-our-greatest-hope?lang=eng.

2. Dieter F. Uchtdorf, "Point of Safe Return," *Ensign*, April 2007, https://www.churchofjesuschrist.org/study/general-conference/2007/04/point-of-safe-return?lang=eng.

3. David A. Bednar, "In the Strength of the Lord," *BYU Speeches*, October 23, 2001, https://speeches.byu.edu/talks/david-a-bednar/strength-lord/.

4. Bednar, "Strength of the Lord."

5. "What Is the Self Coaching Model?" *The Life Coach School*, accessed September 17, 2020, https://thelifecoachschool.com/self-coaching-model-guide/.

6. Doctrine and Covenants 63:34.

7. Robby Berman, "New Study Suggests We Have 6,200 Thoughts Every Day," *Big Think* (blog), July 16, 2020, https://bigthink.com/mind-brain/how-many-thoughts-per-day.

8. Lynn G. Robbins, "Agency and Anger," *Ensign*, April 1998, https://www.churchofjesuschrist.org/study/general-conference/1998/04/agency-and-anger?lang=eng.

9. David A. Bednar, "And Nothing Shall Offend Them," *Ensign*, November 2006, 90, https://www.churchofjesuschrist.org/study/general-conference/2006/10/and-nothing-shall-offend-them?lang=eng.

10. Russell M. Nelson, "Joy and Spiritual Survival," *Ensign*, October 2016, https://www.churchofjesuschrist.org/study/general-conference/2016/10/joy-and-spiritual-survival?lang=eng.

11. David Dickson, "Seven Lies Satan Wants You to Believe," *New Era*, January 2017, https://www.churchofjesuschrist.org/study/new-era/2017/01/seven-lies-satan-wants-you-to-believe?lang=eng.

12. Lynn G. Robbins, "Be 100 Percent Responsible," *BYU Speeches*, August 22, 2017, https://speeches.byu.edu/talks/lynn-g-robbins/be-100-percent-responsible/.

13. Bednar, "Strength of the Lord."

For behold, this is my work
and my glory—to bring to pass
the immortality and eternal life
of man.

Moses 1:39

02. THE LORD'S PLAN

Embracing What Is

The human brain excels at noticing what it doesn't like. Have you noticed? It's on the lookout. The brain is like a computer that is constantly running software called What's Gone Wrong? It's scanning . . . scanning . . . scanning . . . until it locates something—quite easily, I might add. And it seems that we're using this fantastic brain software to gather chapter ideas for the book we are writing, titled *Something Has Gone Wrong*.

First, I notice the dishes in the sink and the Halloween candy wrappers all over the living room floor. Why do I have to do everything around here? From there I jump to the thought that the children are not eating right. They're going to end up with diabetes or a mouth full of cavities. My next thought is that I'm doing a terrible job as a mother, and that's where I usually like to land. With me.

Something is wrong with me.

I'm pretty sure it's true.

My brain software has been collecting proof, and if you have the time, I can share it with you. It's extremely compelling.

According to the experts, in one way or another we all worry that there is something wrong with us. Research professor, author, and speaker Brené Brown says that only sociopaths never question their value.[1] So if, like me, you make most problems mean that there is something wrong with you, then congratulations. You're not a sociopath.

I also have ample evidence that something has gone wrong with my life. It wasn't supposed to look like this. It was supposed to be different. While I'm grateful for parts of it, certain things are just not how I expected them to be. For example, my mother was not supposed to walk off the plane from serving a mission in Kenya with back pain that turned out to be the effect of cancer in her body. That was for sure not in my plan. She was supposed to come home and be with me. Go shopping with me. Come to my kids' soccer games. Pursue the goals she had for herself and spend time with her grandkids and with me. See what I mean? Something has gone wrong.

Perhaps you have similar stories to share from your own book of *Something Has Gone Wrong*. Our chapters all look different, but the main theme is the same for many people's lives. Take these chapter titles, for example:

A good husband would never say that to his wife.
My parents should have loved me better.
I wish our money weren't so tight.
The neighbors have a better life than we do.
I wish my child was active in the Church.
I should get to see my grandkids more often.
My in-laws should be nicer.
My sister shouldn't be so selfish.
The world is a scary place.
I don't want my kids to be sick.

My spouse should have sex with me more often.
My spouse should not want sex so often.
I should have done a better job.
My body should not be so big.
My body should not be so small.
People don't like me.
I just want my kids to be happy.

This is not a fun book. It does not tell an inspiring or motivating story. In fact, it depletes us physically and emotionally, and yet it dominates the way in which many people are viewing their lives. Every chapter in the book is a thought, and these thoughts generate emotions that don't feel good and don't drive us to take useful action. (Remember the model? Thoughts create feelings, and feelings drive actions.)

Some such emotions might include worry, self-pity, resentment, irritation, self-loathing, shame, guilt, discontent, sadness, disappointment, and my personal favorite: frustration. I usually call emotions like these *indulgent*. We indulge in them because it's easier to feel these feelings than it is to override the Something Has Gone Wrong brain software and choose to focus on something different. These indulgent thoughts and feelings are not useful—but the human brain doesn't accept that. It thinks they are important, necessary, and justified. Our brains believe that if we stop thinking about all that has gone wrong, then we are giving in to it and everything will get worse. But as members of the Church, we know about the bigger picture. We believe that we are eternal beings and that coming to earth is a temporary part of God's plan for us to become like Him. We believe that in the premortal existence we made the decision to follow the Lord and come here and that we were excited to have this mortal experience. When we view our lives from this eternal perspective, we are able to think and feel differently about even the most challenging parts of life.

Now, I understand that many things happen in our lives that we don't believe we signed up for. We aren't grateful for these circumstances, and we wouldn't wish them on anyone. But in truth, we *did* sign up for all of it when we chose to come to earth. We knew life here was going to be tough, and we wanted to come anyway. President Dallin H. Oaks said, "In the Council in Heaven, all spirit children of God were introduced to the Father's plan, including its mortal consequences and trials, its heavenly helps, and its glorious destiny. We saw the end from the beginning. All of the myriads of mortals who have been born on this earth chose the Father's plan and fought for it in the heavenly contest that followed."[2]

So we knew our mortal experience would be challenging, and yet we said, *I'm in*? What in the world were we thinking?

For the first seven years of our marriage, my husband and I lived in Huntington Beach in Orange County, California. I loved it there, with its year-round seventy-five-degree weather and beach vibe. And I especially loved that some of the greatest fitness instructors in the country lived there and taught classes at the local gym.

Nolan's class was my favorite. Nolan was high energy and loud music and fun. He was born to be a fitness instructor. I love it when someone taps into their greatness, and this is what Nolan did. When I was kickboxing in his class I felt like Nolan was Jennifer Lopez and I was a back-up dancer. In reality, I was a tired mom with a mom body and mom moves. But that class was a lifeline during a time when I was overwhelmed with two small children, a full-time job, and a shoebox of a rental house.

That hour-long class every Monday evening at six o'clock was like oxygen to me and the other tired moms in our group.

That's right.

Six o'clock: dinner time. It didn't matter. I wasn't going to miss this. Sometimes Nolan would switch off the lights and pass out glow sticks.

I'm not joking.

Glow sticks.

To get a spot in Nolan's class we had to line up a good twenty to thirty minutes early because everyone wanted to get in. But we moms didn't line up just for the fun. Nolan's class was *tough*. We worked hard. Sometimes . . . most times . . . we'd feel like quitting. We weren't sure we could finish. But we'd power through, and afterward our muscles would be on fire and our hearts beating and we'd thank ourselves for persevering and thank Nolan for leading the way.

This is actually the reason we go to the gym, isn't it? We don't not want it to be hard.

I know . . . I used a double negative.

It's not a typo.

Not *not* wanting something is not necessarily the same thing as wanting it. It's just releasing your resistance of the difficult parts. It's being willing to do hard things and knowing that the challenge of your goal is one reason you're doing it. It's even appreciating yourself for getting through the hard and remembering that challenges can transform you. You can do that, you know. Not just with your workout. You can do it with the hard parts of life as well.

Glow sticks and music might help.

Even more helpful, though, is viewing it all through the eternal lens of the Lord's plan. Doing so will help us remember that part of our purpose here on earth is to grow closer to and become more like our Heavenly Parents and that sometimes hardship is required for us to progress. Elder James E. Faust said, "In the pain, the agony, and the heroic endeavors of life, we pass through a refiner's fire, and the insignificant and the unimportant in our lives can melt away like dross and make our faith bright, intact, and strong. In this way the divine image can be mirrored from the soul. It is part of the purging toll exacted of some to become acquainted with God. In the agonies of life, we seem to listen better to the faint, godly whisperings of the Divine Shepherd."[3]

Not only did we agree to come but we actually couldn't wait. According to President Joseph Fielding Smith, "We shouted for joy . . . to have the opportunity of coming to the earth to receive bodies [for we knew] that we might become, through faithfulness, like unto our Father, God."[4] Did you hear that? *We shouted for joy.* I don't know about you, but I haven't shouted for joy about anything in a long time.

Life's challenges strengthen us mentally, spiritually, and emotionally, just as the challenge of a good workout strengthens us physically. And sometimes life enrolls us in tough classes. But if we stop making this mean that something has gone wrong and instead lean on the Lord, we can get through these trials and be stronger as a result. Becoming stronger doesn't take a big trial, either. Sometimes the culmination of many smaller challenges help us progress. But one thing that can get in the way of our progression and keep us stuck in negativity is resistance.

One day, when I was about twenty-seven weeks into my first pregnancy, my doctor said it was time to test me for gestational diabetes. I was not worried about this test at all. My previous medical check-ups had been fine because I was a clean-living, healthy person. I was sure this test would come back negative and we'd check the box and move on. But I was wrong. I hate it when I'm wrong.

The test came back positive.

I had gestational diabetes.

When my doctor called to share the news he calmly said that he would be scheduling a meeting for me at a clinic where nurses and dieticians would teach me how to manage the condition throughout the remainder of my pregnancy. As soon as he said the word *dietician* I knew I was in trouble. I didn't like people telling me what to eat. Especially not a dietician. But I had this baby to think of, so I agreed to go to the appointment.

My first meeting at the clinic was with a kind nurse who drew a diagram on a whiteboard to explain to me and the three other pregnant mamas in attendance how pregnancy hormones sometimes block insulin from moving sugar out of the bloodstream. This information was fascinating and disappointing at the same time. It was tough to hear that this condition was real and that, at minimum, a change in diet and frequent finger pricking was going to be necessary for a while. I didn't love hearing any of this. But one woman in my group was struggling even more than I was.

"Excuse me," she said, "I think there has been a mistake."

The nurse heard her out but didn't seem to believe there'd been a mistake at all.

"I am very healthy and lean. I've always eaten a healthy diet, and I've never been overweight. There's no possible way I have diabetes now."

The nurse assured the woman that her lab results indicated otherwise and that her doctor had referred her to the program to best care for herself and her baby. She explained (again) that gestational diabetes is caused by pregnancy hormones and can happen for women of many different shapes, sizes, and levels of health.

This woman was not having it.

At this point in my life I didn't know the model, but I did by my third and fourth pregnancies, during which I also developed gestational diabetes and went through similar programs where I saw women have the same reactions as that first woman I observed in the clinic that day. Here was her model:

Circumstance: Lab result positive for gestational diabetes.

Thought: Diabetes is something unhealthy people get, and I'm very healthy.

Feeling: Resistant.

Action: Explain to nurses and others that this is a mistake. Tune out when learning about this phenomenon and possible treatment plans. Insist that I don't need this. Don't fully commit to recommendations made by doctors and nurses.

Result: I am not taking care of my own health or the health of my baby.

See how the thought connects to the result? As soon as this mom-to-be got upset because someone told her she was "unhealthy" in some way and she moved into resistance, she ended up with a result she probably didn't want. In this case, the result could prevent her from optimal health for herself and her baby. But this is what the brain does when we really don't want something to be true (even though it is true after all).

It resists.

Our brain believes that if we accept reality, then we are giving in and allowing it—as though resisting the situation and being mad about it is somehow preventing it. Now listen up, friend. If I thought that you resisting certain things (even

44

what we want to call "bad" things) would prevent them from happening, I'd be right there with you kicking and screaming about the injustice of it all.

But that doesn't work.

Denying that we received an unwanted diagnosis doesn't make it go away. That's not to say we shouldn't get a second and third opinion. Or that we wouldn't want to do everything in our power to change our health condition or fight a disease. Resistance is not those things. Resistance is when we pout and sulk and refuse to acknowledge reality. Instead, we can learn to embrace life—the joyful parts and the terrible parts.

No, really.

We can embrace that we are supposed to suffer and struggle and get bad news sometimes. Embrace that sometimes people will disappoint us, plans will fall through, and downright terrible things will happen to us and to people we love. Embrace that even though something has gone wrong, nothing has actually gone wrong in the eternal picture. Resistance doesn't prevent trials, it just adds more negative emotion on top of the negative emotion we already have (and might want to keep) about the bad news.

Embracing all parts of life doesn't mean that you don't allow for grief. Grief (even the resistance portion) is necessary when things don't go the way we thought they would. But don't stay in resistance. Don't add another chapter to your sad book. At some point, when you're sick and tired of feeling sick and tired, choose to feel something different. Christ's Atonement can help us do this. We can pray to have an eternal perspective. We can pray for strength beyond our natural abilities to handle challenges, process grief or pain, and move through a trial. We can be made stronger through Christ as we are reminded in

Matthew 19:26: "With men this is impossible; but with God all things are possible."

The woman at the gestational diabetes clinic wasn't wrong or weak. She just didn't realize that resistance is an emotion that feels useful but only blocks our ability to move through a difficult situation rather than pressing against it as it forges its way through our lives. This might be a more useful model for her situation:

> **Circumstance:** Lab result positive for gestational diabetes.
> **Thought:** I wasn't expecting that, but tell me more.
> **Feeling:** Surprised and open.
> **Action:** Allow for the disappointment or fear I might feel. Be curious about what the doctors and nurses tell me. Study more about this diagnosis. Commit to taking care of myself and my baby. Pray for strength and wisdom.
> **Result:** I adjust to a circumstance I wasn't expecting.

Again, we can have acceptance but still have pain, disappointment, sadness, grief, or even fear. But when we accept our reality, we don't add resistance on top of those emotions and make them unbearable and prevent ourselves from showing up the way we want to in our lives. With acceptance, we have access to our best problem-solving and creative-solution-finding abilities. We become more flexible and open. We even make room to hear the Spirit. Accepting challenges is easier when we keep an eternal perspective and when we remember that the hardships we experience are not an indicator that something has gone wrong but are in fact a necessary part of the plan. President M. Russell Ballard said:

> I can understand why someone who lacks eternal perspective might see the horrifying news footage of starving

children and man's inhumanity to man and shake a fist at the heavens and cry, "If there is a God, how could he allow such things to happen?"

The answer is not easy, but it isn't that complicated either. God has put his plan in motion. It proceeds through natural laws that are, in fact, God's laws. Since they are his, he is bound by them as are we. I recognize for purposes we mortals may not understand, the Lord can control the elements. For the most part, however, he does not cause but he allows nature to run its course. In this imperfect world, bad things sometimes happen.[5]

Accepting challenging circumstances doesn't mean we won't try to influence our lives and the lives of others for good. It only means that we are more effective and at peace when we accept our trials from a peaceful, eternal perspective.

Humans are not capable of operating from resentment and acceptance at the same time. We can't simultaneously be in fear and in love. We are either in openness, compassion, and curiosity around the people and events in our lives, or we are in resistance, judgment, and shut-down. We can't be in both camps at once. The brain doesn't work that way.[6] Christ was, of course, the perfect example of this concept. Even as He suffered tremendous pain, He said, "Father, if thou be willing, remove this cup from me: nevertheless not my will, but thine, be done."[7] His sacrifice is the ultimate example of not resisting, even when it was a challenge beyond what any of us can imagine.

When my kindergartner, Oliver, started school this year, he had to take the school bus. All of the neighborhood kids ride the bus, and I knew that, due to our work schedules, I would eventually want him to ride it too. So, while I considered driving him for his first year of school, I worried that if he didn't learn the bus routine as a kindergartner, when the teachers and bus drivers are extra attentive, it would be even harder next year. Bring on the bus.

Oliver gets nervous leaving my side when it's time to go to Primary at church, even though he's been doing it for three years. He doesn't like unpredictability or being without a designated adult to watch over him. Riding the bus involves some unpredictability, and Oliver didn't like it one bit. He wanted to know exactly who he would be sitting by. He wanted to know who would be there to greet him when the bus got to school. He wanted to know who would walk him to his class line and what would happen when it was time to come home. I didn't want Oliver to be anxious, so I tried to control the world. No biggie.

I'm seriously good at manipulating the world around me.

Or so I like to believe.

I found fifth-grade girls from our ward who are triplets and who rode his same bus. It was brilliant. They agreed to help Oliver on the bus, and if one of them was sick, I thought, there would still be two more available. I also went to the school and found out as much as I could about the before- and after-school routines, and then I explained it all to Oliver. I tried desperately to prevent him from feeling afraid and from crying as he got on the bus, but do you know what?

It didn't work.

He cried every day about the bus, and not just for the first week. We are about three months into school as I write this, and Oliver is still in tears most days.

I resisted this reality, and I resisted it pretty hard. Controlling the world wasn't working, and I was not happy that Oliver was upset about getting on the bus every day. Who would be? It felt important and useful to not want him to cry every morning.

It even seemed like the motherly thing to do, feeling irritated about all of this. I tried to talk him into not being afraid, and I tried to bribe him into being brave. I essentially taught him that he should resist what he was feeling and fight back the tears.

Have you ever tried to not cry when the tears were coming? If so, you know what happens. You want to cry even more, and when you finally do it's like releasing the floodgates of a dam. This was my model:

> **Circumstance:** Oliver is crying while walking to the bus stop.
> **Thought:** I don't want him to cry.
> **Feeling:** Irritated.
> **Action:** Try to talk him out of it. Try to set up preventative measures that sometimes work but often do not. Bribe him to not cry, which he is unable to do. Be grumpy about having to deal with all of this. Worry.
> **Result:** I am crying inside. I want Oliver to stop crying so I can stop "crying."

Again, notice how my thought ended up in my result line. One day a few weeks ago I realized that I was not happy with my reaction to Oliver's crying, and, knowing that I am always the creator of my results, I reluctantly shifted from trying to control Oliver to observing myself. I am often reluctant to do this. Becoming conscious of my thoughts and understanding how they are affecting my actions takes some energy and focus. So, don't feel bad if you need some time to be willing to take a look at yourself. I sometimes try everything else first, even though I know better. But once I shifted my focus and discovered the model I just showed you, I realized that I was resisting reality and that the result was not working for me. This wasn't how I wanted to show up for my son.

That's when I decided to step back and look at things from an eternal perspective.

I had to play with my story and be slow with it, though. Because when I shift to a new model, I have to be willing to be wrong. I have to be wrong about all the painful thoughts I've been thinking, so my brain initially rejects the new model. I just keep playing with the possibility and stay open while I ask myself a lot of questions: What if I'm wrong about all of this? What if nothing has gone wrong here? What if Oliver is supposed to be scared? What if he's having the exact experience in this life that he needs to be having? What if I didn't *not* want him to cry? The answer to these questions is, of course, Then I would feel peaceful about all of this. Initially my brain comes back at me with, "Yeah, but that's ridiculous. Of course he shouldn't be scared," and I just keep the questions alive: I know, but what if I'm wrong about that? What if he just needs to be scared right now?

Eventually I got to a more useful model:

Circumstance: Oliver is crying while walking to the bus stop.

Thought: Maybe he wants or needs to be scared.

Feeling: Open.

Action: I tell him it's OK to cry if he wants to. I tell him I'm very proud of him for getting on that school bus whether he's crying or not. I tell him that I love him and Heavenly Father loves him and that I feel afraid sometimes too and there is nothing wrong with feeling that way.

Result: I connect with my sweet Oliver, and I am being the mom I want to be. In short, I'm OK so I can be more present for Oliver.

This change illustrates the power of remembering that we are here on earth to struggle occasionally and accepting this reality for ourselves and our children. Notice that I didn't get all the way to the thought "I'm so glad he is crying," and I wouldn't want to. I still want to be disappointed and sad when my child is sad. But I have now dropped the resistance. I'm just embracing the fact that this is a hard situation for Oliver and for me and that we can do hard things. As I've shifted my thinking, I've seen more clearly how this experience is refining Oliver and me. I believe that allowing the emotions we feel as we progress through challenges is part of a healthy human experience. If Oliver needs to cry, I genuinely want him to do so without feeling ashamed or tightening up against it. There's nothing wrong with crying.

I'm also grateful he's having experiences that could help him gain confidence as he overcomes hardship. He might learn to be more compassionate with others who struggle. Oliver's anxiety about riding the bus provides opportunities for me to teach Oliver about prayer and the comfort of the Spirit. The reality is that the characteristics we want our kids to develop don't come from ease. They come through facing challenges. So, in some ways, I'm grateful for all of this.

One morning when we arrived at the bus stop, Oliver's triplets were not there because they had early morning violin practice. Oliver was extra nervous. We were running a bit late, so the other kids had already boarded the bus when we ran up to the door just before it pulled away. Oliver was sobbing with anxiety. The door squeaked open and Mr. Al the bus driver leaned out and said, "Hey Oliver, Hayden is right here waiting to sit by you." Oliver sighed with relief, and now I was the one fighting back tears. I didn't know that Mr. Al knew Oliver's name. I had no idea who Hayden was. I found out later that she is a fourth-grade girl who has been helping Oliver when the triplets are gone. My heart could have burst with gratitude. And that was just the beginning. We've had many more experiences, even tender mercies, as people have rallied around Oliver this year at the bus stop. For this I am so grateful.

Even with my mother's cancer I'm working to accept what is rather than resisting reality.

It's not easy.

I have to work at it.

I also feel significant pain about it, and I want to keep that pain.

But in the suffering there is a peace that is challenging to put into words. Sometimes I still resist accepting that my mother is sick. But most days I can find many tender mercies surrounding this trial. For example, through a series of seemingly random events, my family and I ended up moving near my parents. I haven't lived near them since I graduated high school, but an unexpected change in my husband's job brought me home. The same week we arrived, the doctor told my mother she had cancer.

Elder Dieter F. Uchtdorf said, "Sooner or later, I believe that all of us experience times when the very fabric of our world tears at the seams, leaving us feeling alone, frustrated, and adrift. It can happen to anyone. No one is immune. Everyone's situation is different, and the details of each life are unique. Nevertheless, I have learned that there is something that would take away the bitterness that may come into our lives. There is one thing we can do to make life sweeter, more joyful, even glorious. We can be grateful!"[8]

I have felt a great deal of gratitude along with the sorrow as I've tried to keep an eternal perspective. Gratitude that I can be here to spend time with my mom and help my parents out in some small way. Gratitude that it's never been easier to love her. Gratitude that she has my dad around to care for her. Gratitude for the peace that comes with knowing that God has a plan for all of us. Gratitude for the increased patience and love I have for all humans because I know we are all suffering in some way.

Experiences like these change us and are part of why we're here on earth.

Layering Emotions

We humans are fascinating creatures. I love studying people because I never get bored and I never have us all figured out. I can't wait for the day when I better understand how we were created and why we are the way we are, but until that day I'll take the small insights we have and the observations I notice. For example, I've noticed that humans do what I call *layering emotions*. We think a thought and feel an emotion (let's say it's a negative one), and then we begin thinking more thoughts that go nicely with the original thought, which creates even more negative emotion. This cycle goes on until we've layered all sorts of emotions, and then we say that we've had a rough day.

Several months ago, I was out of town when I got a text message from one of my kids. It read, "Where is the first aid kit?"

Um . . . *what*?

My model:

Circumstance: Text message from my child asks, "Where is the first aid kit?"

Thought: Someone is hurt.

Feeling: Worry.

Action: Text back: "WAIT. What's wrong? Who is hurt?" Try calling. Then text again. Then call again. Then text and call and text and call. Begin creating horror stories in my head about what happened.

Result: I'm convinced someone is hurt, and I'm hurting inside as well.

It must be the dog. He bit my daughter's face and she is bleeding profusely and even if she survives she will have no face for the rest of her life, and it will be my fault for leaving town. Here comes guilt. Let's layer that on top of worry. I should never leave town. Never leave the house even. Also, the dog has to go.

Call again. No answer. Text again. No reply.

Wait, maybe someone fell off the trampoline. I knew it would happen eventually. My husband, Jake, never wanted that trampoline because he said they are dangerous, and now he's right. I should have listened to him. My son fell off and his bone is protruding from his leg and the kids are freaking out and the ambulance is on the way but Jake told them to get the first aid kit because Jake can fix anything and anyone so he's going to see what he can do. Bone protruding. Blood. Screams. My fault. I should have listened to Jake. More guilt. Let's pile it on.

Ring. Ring. Ring. Voicemail. Why won't they answer me? Let's add frustration too.

Now I'm in a panic due to the horror story in my head about what's happening at home.

These things could happen, you know. Things like this happen every day. But of course none of these things *did* happen on the day I got that text message. One of my kids just needed a Band-Aid for a small cut, and she couldn't find the Band-Aids, but I didn't know that because nobody was replying to my calls or messages. Turns out they found the Band-Aids.

Notice that my first emotion was worry. Then I layered on guilt because every story I came up with included some version of why this was my fault. It always comes back to me, for better or for worse. It's the curse of being a human: we think everything is about us. And then there was frustration when nobody was answering my calls or texts. Worry + guilt + frustration = panic.

Layering negative emotions is not useful, but we do it all the time. We do it automatically. We can work to minimize this phenomenon, but that's not my point here. My point is that if we can layer negative emotions and intensify the negativity, then we can also layer positive emotions and intensify the positivity. What if we layer on as many positive emotions as possible? What would happen?

I'll tell you what happens.

You get to pure bliss.

Pure joy.

Pure love.

The best feelings on the planet are available to us if we keep layering on positive emotions when we feel good. Guilt is the easiest negative layering emotion, but there is a go-to emotion for positivity as well. It's gratitude. Positive feelings you have in any situation will be compounded if you layer some gratitude right on top. Just like food tastes even better when you add a little seasoning or chocolate or ranch dressing, life gets better and you feel happier when you add gratitude.

Feeling excited about a girls' night out this weekend? Great. Now add gratitude. Gratitude for your friends. Gratitude that you have a husband who can watch the kids so you can go. Gratitude ahead of time for the fun evening you're going to make sure you have. Gratitude to yourself for taking care of you in this way. Gratitude to Heavenly Parents for the experience of being alive. Pretty soon you'll be feeling more than a flash of anticipation; you'll be experiencing something deeper and more long-lasting. We might call it joy. Because after all, we are here on earth not only to overcome challenges. In 2 Nephi we learn more about the great plan of happiness. We learn that we are meant for joy.[9]

Gratitude is not just something we *should* do. It's not a commandment we've been given because the Lord needs us to thank Him or because it might make other people feel good when we say *thank you*. It's for us. If we put gratitude in our model's feeling line we get the kinds of actions and results we want in our lives. Actions like kindness, appreciation, and enjoyment lead to the result of experiencing life and the world how we want to experience them. But you'll have to choose to be grateful because your brain software that constantly scans for problems is strong. You'll have to look for the blessings you are already grateful for and not take them for granted. From time to time, pause to notice these good things. You'll then get to feel gratitude, which feels amazing.

The Something Has Gone Wrong brain software is not going to get turned off completely, and we wouldn't want it to be. That software keeps us away from fires and dark alleys, and it stops us from posting our political opinions in all caps on Instagram. It's a useful part of the brain, and if you're willing to supervise it, you can gain more authority over your problems and increase joy in your life.

The truth is that nothing has gone wrong. We know this because loving Heavenly Parents sent us here to earth so we could have experiences that would allow us to become like Them. Do you know which experiences allow us to become like Them? The hard ones. The ones that we weren't expecting. The ones we wouldn't choose if we were writing our own story. I'm not sure why we think that things should go smoothly for us and for all the people we love, because do you know who never has problems?

That's right.

Nobody.

Problems are part of the plan.

Problems are the good part. They give us the chance to examine ourselves and choose whether we're going to stay stuck or take charge of what we think and who we are. We can become our highest selves only when we are up against a challenge. Otherwise there is no growth.

Let's be grateful. Let's say yes to all of it. Let's let go of resistance to what is, and let's layer on as much gratitude as we can.

Nothing has gone wrong.

I promise.

---

1. Brené Brown, "Listening to Shame," March 2012, TED video, 20:23 (quote at 14:50), https://www.ted.com/talks/brene_brown_listening_to_shame?language=en.

2. Dallin H. Oaks, "The Great Plan," *Ensign*, April 2020, https://www.churchofjesuschrist.org/study/general-conference/2020/04/51oaks?lang=eng.

3. James E. Faust, "The Refiner's Fire," *Ensign*, April 1979, https://www.churchofjesuschrist.org/study/general-conference/1979/04/the-refiners-fire?lang=eng.

4. Joseph Fielding Smith, *Man, His Origin and Destiny* (1965), 277, as quoted in Robert D. Hales, "To Act for Ourselves: The Gift and Blessings of Agency," *Ensign*, April 2006, https://www.churchofjesuschrist.org/study/general-conference/2006/04/to-act-for-ourselves-the-gift-and-blessings-of-agency?lang=eng.

5. M. Russell Ballard, "Answers to Life's Questions," *Ensign*, April 1995, https://www.churchofjesuschrist.org/study/general-conference/1995/04/answers-to-lifes-questions?lang=eng.

6. Nancy Colier, LCSW, Rev., "Choosing Love Not Fear," *Psychology Today*, February 22, 2018, https://www.psychologytoday.com/us/blog/inviting-monkey-tea/201802/choosing-love-not-fear.

7. Luke 22:42.

8. Dieter F. Uchtdorf, "Grateful in Any Circumstances," *Ensign*, May 2014, 70–77, https://www.churchofjesuschrist.org/study/general-conference/2014/04/grateful-in-any-circumstances?lang=eng.

9. 2 Nephi 2:25.

Therefore, cheer up your hearts,
and remember that ye are free
to act for yourselves.

2 Nephi 10:23

03. AGENCY

The Ultimate Plan

Other people. They don't do it right. Am I right?

From where I'm sitting, I can see clearly how other people should live their lives. For example, I can see how my parents could be happier if my dad didn't get so defensive when my mom gives him a suggestion and if my mom would just stop giving my dad suggestions in the first place. It's simple. But they don't do this. They do whatever they want instead. Come on, Mom and Dad.

Or my kids. It's simple: arrive on your due date, be a well-behaved child, choose the right, love everyone, be confident and happy, study and work hard, read your scriptures, stay away from the naughty kids, brush your teeth, date nice people, take care of your body, go to college, get married in the temple, live close to me and your dad forever, have babies so I can be a grandma, and then we all basically live happily ever after. It's not rocket science, kids. Just do what I tell you.

But something has thrown a wrench in my perfect plans for the people I love. It's their agency. They have the ability to choose.

And so will their spouses and their children one day. I can only imagine how this will complicate my plans. When I was growing up in the Church and learned about the importance of agency, I nodded my head in agreement and thought, "Yes, of course. Agency is an important and necessary part of God's plan." But I was mostly thinking about my own agency—I wasn't thinking that other people should be able to behave however they want to, especially if what they want to do is terrible.

But they should.

And they can.

And they do.

Agency is part of what makes the Lord's plan different from Satan's plan, isn't it? In Moses 4:3 we read, "Wherefore, because that Satan rebelled against me, and sought to destroy the agency of man, which I, the Lord God, had given him, and also, that I should give unto him mine own power; by the power of mine Only Begotten, I caused that he should be cast down."

I regularly find myself pointing out to my clients the fact that everyone has agency. The conversation typically starts with a story about someone behaving in a way that my client doesn't like. Let's just take this example about my client's sister-in-law because, according to my experience coaching women, there is an abundance of difficult sisters-in-law in this world. The fact that I don't have one makes me wonder if I'm my family's difficult sister-in-law. That could be. At any rate, my client Emily once told me that her sister-in-law Jessica was irresponsible with money. Jessica had said that she couldn't afford to come to the family reunion, but Emily noticed that she spent money on clothes, home remodels, and other things she didn't really need. Emily was pretty sure that Jessica and her husband were in too much debt, and she believed it was irresponsible.

We think we know how other people should manage their money, but I'm pretty sure we don't. Because if it's true that people should do what we want instead of what they want, then we are making a case against agency. We'll come back to Emily and Jessica, but let's look at some other examples first.

Maybe it's a child who talks to her parents in a disrespectful way. Or a child who is vaping. Or a child who is failing math, who won't get a job, who has decided not to serve a mission, or who has decided to leave the Church. You get the idea. Kids should make the wise choices we've laid out for them, right? Or perhaps not. Because, again, agency. But if we take a step back and remember that other people are supposed to have agency and that we are all going to make mistakes, then we can begin to see the brilliance of the entire plan and understand how to find peace for ourselves along our journey.

I recently worked with a woman, Julia, whose husband had decided that he no longer wanted to be an active member of the Church. Julia felt that his decision was unfair. It felt like a violation of the agreement she and her husband had made years ago when they were married and sealed in the temple. She had some pain that I would call clean pain, and I encouraged her to allow and lean into that pain. *Clean pain* is the type of pain we feel when we are going through a grieving process over what we thought would be.[1] Julia's pain was coming from thoughts like, "This is disappointing. I'm heartbroken. I wasn't expecting this. I'm afraid of what will happen next." Allowing that kind of pain would move Julia though this experience.

But she had other pain that I would call *dirty pain*. This pain was unnecessary, and it would keep her stuck if she let it. It was coming from thoughts like, "This isn't fair. He can't do this. This was not supposed to happen. He owes me. He needs to figure this out." These thoughts, while tempting to believe, go against the idea that every one of us has agency—specifically, in this case, Julia's husband. Experiencing dirty pain is not wrong. But it's helpful to notice that this type of thinking is not as useful as our brains believe it to be.

I'll be honest. At one point in my life I had to wrestle with the idea of agency being the best way. I understood that Satan wanted the glory instead of giving it to Heavenly Father,[2] and that didn't sound right, but I felt that we could have spent more time considering the idea that everyone chooses the right all the time. I mean, my unsupervised brain really believes that forcing others to make good choices would be better than letting them make terrible choices like they do. Obviously. But my brain is wrong about that. President M. Russell Ballard said, "We tend to think of agency as a personal matter. . . . We forget that agency offers the same privilege of choice to others. At times we will be affected adversely by the way other people choose to exercise their agency. Our Heavenly Father feels so strongly about protecting our agency that he allows his children to exercise it, either for good or for evil."[3]

When I tell a client that her child is supposed to experience hard things, to make wrong choices, and even to suffer sometimes as a result of those choices, I never get a reply of, "Oh yeah, I forgot about agency for a minute, but thanks for the reminder! I feel great now!"

But here's what I have come to believe as I've pondered this principle: Agency is of utmost importance. Next to the Atonement of Jesus Christ, it might be the most critical part of the plan of salvation. Elder Robert D. Hales said, "Agency is the catalyst that leads us to express our inward spiritual desires in outward Christlike behavior. Agency permits us to make faithful, obedient choices that strengthen us so that we can lift and strengthen others. Agency used righteously allows light to dispel the darkness and enables us to live with joy and happiness in the present, look with faith to the future, even into the eternities, and not dwell on the things of the past. Our use of agency determines who we are and what we will be."[4]

In other words, agency is why living here on earth is the best way for us to become like our Heavenly Parents. Agency makes this life challenging, and challenge is necessary for our learning and growth. It requires that we pay attention to our thoughts and actions so we can achieve the things we desire in this life and in the next. It gives us the opportunity to overcome our primitive, animal brains in the name of our future, highest good. Making the best choices requires practice, and sometimes we won't choose the right. Sometimes we'll choose the easier, more immediate pleasure or we'll confuse ourselves about the way to find peace. But our agency makes this life the Ivy League curriculum that it is.

I have a few friends who graduated from Ivy League universities. I admire those friends tremendously. Imagine if at those schools someone had sat next to them in class, whispering the right answers into their ears the entire time they attended. Every test. Every paper. Obviously, that would have negated their experience and their learning. In reality, my friends had to struggle, make mistakes, and be committed enough to learn the material and do well, even though that was the hard way. That tough experience is what makes their education invaluable.

Because of agency every choice we make, whether we follow Christ or not, creates an opportunity for us to evolve. When we choose to follow Christ, we are strengthening our ability to make decisions from our highest self, and sometimes this means foregoing immediate pleasure. When we choose to go against His teachings, we experience natural consequences that again provide us with an opportunity to exercise agency. Once we end up wherever we end up as a result of our choices, we have more choices to make. What now? What will we do with the challenges we have now created for ourselves? Will we succumb to shame and overwhelm, or will we remember that we can make a different choice anytime we want to? Elder Hales has spoken about this part of our agency:

> If, through our unrighteous choices, we have lost our footing on that path, we must remember the agency we were given, agency we may choose to exercise again. I speak especially to those overcome by the thick darkness of addiction. If you have fallen into destructive, addictive behaviors, you may feel that you are spiritually in a black hole. As with real black holes in space, it may seem all but impossible for light to penetrate to where you are. How do you escape? I testify the only way is through the very agency you exercised so valiantly in your premortal life, the agency that the adversary cannot take away without your yielding it to him.[5]

I know this part of agency all too well.

It was a hot Tuesday night in June when I sat up in my bed with tears streaming down my face. I was sweating from the lack of air conditioning in our Huntington Beach duplex. The ocean breeze was nice and all, but that breeze didn't make it into our shoebox of a house.

Sweating and crying.

How had I let my life get to this point?

I'd woken up sobbing because of a nightmare. I was in a helicopter all by myself out over the middle of the ocean. It was raining and the sky was full of lightning. The ocean was violent with wind and waves, and I was going to crash. I was lost and alone with no sign of land in sight, and I was filled with fear. I was going to die. Alone. It was terrifying.

Waking from the dream was a relief but only slightly. I wasn't actually going to die in a helicopter over the ocean, but I knew where the dream was coming from. I'd been filled with shame, fear, and confusion for months now over decisions I had made that went against the things I believed and the values I'd been taught. I didn't even recognize myself. I didn't know what to do next. I felt too far gone to be honest with myself or anyone else, and the anxiety was now creeping into my dreams.

I'm not going to go into detail about the choices that led me to this point. What I will say is that the Spirit had left me, or so I thought. My choices had separated me from the Spirit, and I had made them knowingly. I knew better. Many times I had wanted to sink into despair, but that night I felt the Spirit give me a tap on the shoulder. The Lord will keep trying to get through to us even when we've made it tough for ourselves to hear Him. He'll keep trying to speak to us. We may have to wake up crying and sweating and desperate for relief before we can hear Him, but He will never give up on us.

This tap on my shoulder came in the form of a thought: "You don't have to keep suffering like this. You know what to do." And I did know. I knew I needed to go talk to my bishop, I needed to seek professional help, and I needed to go through a difficult repentance process. I knew it was going to get harder before it got easier. But I knew I could use my agency to head in a new direction any time I wanted to. I knew all of this was true. And I had finally exhausted myself enough that I did just that.

When we make choices, we face consequences. When we make foolish choices like I had, we may negatively impact our health, our financial situation, our relationships, our self-image, our freedom, or any number of other areas. Consequences are real. But we never lose our agency. Even if we are locked up in a jail cell, we still have agency. We always get to choose who we will be. We get to decide how we will think about things, and our thoughts will eventually create a result for us.

I had used my agency to head down a dark alley of sorts. And I walked further and further down it for a long time. Eventually I realized that when I was ready, I could turn and head out into the sunlight. It took me a while to find sunlight, but all it took was one decision to get started in that direction. And while that experience was challenging, a part of me values it tremendously because of the person I had to become to get through it and because of the relationship I have with Christ as a result. This is the power of agency and of Christ's Atonement. Thanks to the Spirit and my knowledge of the principle of agency, this became my new model:

Circumstance: Decisions I made in the past.

Thought: I can make a different choice anytime I want.

Feeling: Empowered.

Action: I begin thinking about making better choices. I open up to the grace of Christ's Atonement. I feel comforted by the Holy Ghost.

Result: I begin heading in a better direction.

I hate to break it to you, but you, your family and friends, your kids, and everyone else on planet Earth are supposed to sometimes make mistakes, and even to sometimes suffer tremendously as a result of those mistakes. It's painful, but it's also OK. Nothing has gone wrong here because when Heavenly Father sent us to earth and told us to keep the commandments, He knew that because of our agency we would make mistakes.

As members of the Church we have learned the importance of agency in God's plan. Now I'm simply suggesting we use that knowledge to improve our own lives. We must get better at focusing more on controlling our own agency and less on trying to control that of others. Because the people in our lives can do whatever they want.

Really.

Whatever they want.

The people you love have agency. But so do you. The question I recommend you ask is not, "How can I get that person to behave better?" but, "Who do I want to be now?"

Choosing Your Focus

We can be so focused on how other people are using their agency that we neglect to consider how we want to use ours. We can delegate our choices to the automatic, unconscious part of our brain and just react to life and the people around us, or we can deliberately choose who we will be in any given circumstance.

Heavenly Father wants us to use our agency for good. He expects us to act, not to be acted upon.[6] The question "Who do I want to be?" is not always easy to answer, but it is an extremely useful one to ask—especially when others utilize their agency in a way we don't approve of. Let's take a look at our examples again, using the model to help us gain awareness of ourselves. Let's begin with Emily, whose sister-in-law Jessica is being "foolish" with her money.

Circumstance: Jessica is in debt.

Thought: She should be more responsible with her money.

Feeling: Judgmental.

Action: Ruminate on the situation, gossip about it to others in the family, be less than genuine in my interactions with her, disconnect from her in various ways.

Result: I'm really not being the kind of person I want to be.

Yes, Jessica might be making her own life harder by not managing her money well. But that's her business. What if Emily stayed out of Jessica's business? What if Emily decided to keep the focus on her own agency and how she wanted to use it? We get to decide if we are going to judge others or love them. We can be critical or curious. Who do you want to be? That question that will direct you to considering your own agency and away from trying to control others.

While our brains believe judgment is useful, unless we are using it to truly protect ourselves in some way, it's not. It separates us from one another, it does not control the subject of our judgment, and it is not our natural state. Judgment is our earthly state. Our natural state is love and compassion and kindness because we're created in God's image,[7] and God is love. We will never feel good when we're judging in this way. This is the real problem. The problem isn't someone else's actions or bank account. That's outside of us. What's inside of us is the source of our problems.

To get to a more peaceful place, we need to ask ourselves who we want to be. What kind of sister-in-law do I want to be to my sister-in-law who is in debt? What kind of woman in the world do I want to be? The truth is, I want to be loving and non-judgmental and kind and open. I want to be someone my sister-in-law would feel comfortable coming to for advice or help with money if she wanted that, and I want to be a supportive influence in her life. If she doesn't want help or advice (which right now she doesn't . . . trust me), then I just want to enjoy her and put my brain to work thinking about a problem or challenge that is more useful than this one—a problem or challenge that is mine to own. Maybe it's starting a hobby or a business or solving the homeless problem downtown or figuring out how to get out of cooking dinner ever again. Seriously. There are so many more useful things I could put my brain to work on, rather than my sister-in-law's problem, which is actually none of my business. Here's a new model for Emily:

> **Circumstance:** Jessica is in debt.
>
> **Thought:** She gets to do whatever she wants with her money, and I love her.
>
> **Feeling:** Open.
>
> **Action:** I don't think about her money (so I get to think about something more useful instead). I notice the things I love about Jessica, and I have more meaningful conversations with her because I'm actually listening and genuinely curious about her.
>
> **Result:** I like who I'm being, and I love my sister-in-law.

Remember Julia, whose husband left the Church? Julia and I did many models together. She slowly began taking accountability for the result she was creating for herself instead of giving the credit to her husband. Her original model looked like this:

> **Circumstance:** My husband hasn't gone to church in three years.
>
> **Thought:** He needs to come back to church for me to be happy.
>
> **Feeling:** Victimized.
>
> **Action:** Try to get him to come back to church. Feel sorry for myself. Judge him for his choices. Resent him for his decisions.
>
> **Result:** I need to "come back to church."

This model helped Julia realize that she was not able to feel the Spirit in her own life. She saw that she was full of fear, not faith. She was not the Christlike, loving person she wanted to be. And that's a problem—not because Julia *should* be more Christlike but because Julia's peace of mind and happiness are available to her but she wasn't accessing them. It turns out that being Christlike is what feels the best to us, although the people around us probably prefer it as well. Julia couldn't get out of this trap while she believed she was a victim. But over time, as she observed how her thinking was poisoning her experience, her marriage, and her relationship with God, she used her agency to make a different choice. She decided to believe that her husband's decisions were not hers to manage and to instead be the kind of wife she wanted to be regardless of his choices. Her first step was to shift into curiosity—genuine curiosity. We created a model that she felt she could get to at times. It looked like this:

Circumstance: My husband hasn't gone to church in three years.

Thought: I wonder what it's like for him right now.

Feeling: Curious.

Action: Ask him what he believes about God. Ask him what he's feeling and experiencing. Listen to him with compassion. Be a safe place for him to be vulnerable. Practice self-care and get help for myself as well when needed.

Result: I like who I'm being much better.

This is only one of the many models that Julia and I worked on together. It was important for us to do models on Julia's thoughts about herself as well. This work is not about being a martyr or tolerating mistreatment or even staying in a marriage that you may not want to stay in. I want you to make the decision that is the most loving toward everyone in the story, including you. Cleaning up your thinking and taking ownership of your emotions and results helps you feel the Spirit and connect with God so you can know what decisions you should make in your life. It also gives you the confidence to make difficult decisions. Be the person you want to be and then ask the Lord what you should do.

And as a side note, my work deals in the realm of common problems in functional relationships, but sometimes there are situations that go beyond these types of challenges. The same principles apply, but I want to be extremely clear: Please don't allow other people to mistreat you. Use your agency to get away from abusive situations. Agency means that people can and will behave terribly at times. Agency also means that we don't have to tolerate that behavior. If you are in a dangerous or abusive situation, stop waiting for the other person to change. Use your agency to protect yourself—get away and seek help if necessary.

Now, listen. I know that accepting other people's agency no matter what is easier said than done. If you think I calmly walk around all day allowing people to make their own choices and never try desperately to control them, think again. And anyone who tells you that you can't control your children doesn't know about licorice, toys, screen time, phones, or use of the car as bargaining tools. I'm not a parenting expert, so please don't think I'm saying you *should* use these things to attempt to control your child. I'm simply admitting that sometimes I do this, for better or for worse.

Even if you're not in a position of authority or in the mood to bribe, we human beings can influence one another with our example, with our words, or in many other ways. We should be conscious of the influence we have on others. But I promise you that if you notice when you're feeling like a victim, feeling overly frustrated, feeling resentful, or feeling stuck, you can stop blaming others and take responsibility for the thoughts you're thinking. Because those thoughts are *always* the reason for your suffering.

This is wonderful news. Because while we may be able to influence our spouses, our friends, and even our teenagers, we cannot actually control them. Again, this doesn't mean I will never try to do so at times. In fact, if I ever figure out how to control people, then I will ditch this book and write that one instead. Trust me. But I do believe that God is incredibly wise in fully honoring our agency, even knowing that we will hurt ourselves and create problems for each other at times. When I'm really managing my brain, I let go of focusing on everyone else and turn the focus toward myself, which of course helps me find peace.

When everything is going smoothly and the people around us behave just as we expected they would, there is nothing to push back against; therefore, there is no opportunity to use our agency for our own growth. When challenges occur, we have choices to make—our choices. If we keep the focus on our choices, it doesn't mean we won't experience pain. It means that pain can refine us, as it's supposed to, and that we can evolve for the better because of it.

---

1. Martha Beck, "Emotional Pain: How Do I Cope With This?" *HER: Women's Health and Wellness* (blog), https://www.empowher.com/mental-health/content/emotional-pain-how-do-i-cope-martha-beck.

2. Moses 4:1, 3.

3. M. Russell Ballard, "Answers to Life's Questions," *Ensign*, April 1995, https://www.churchofjesuschrist.org/study/general-conference/1995/04/answers-to-lifes-questions?lang=eng.

4. Robert D. Hales, "To Act for Ourselves: The Gift and Blessings of Agency," *Ensign*, April 2006, https://www.churchofjesuschrist.org/study/general-conference/2006/04/to-act-for-ourselves-the-gift-and-blessings-of-agency?lang=eng.

5. Hales, "To Act for Ourselves."

6. 2 Nephi 2:26.

7. Moses 2:27.

TIME OUT FOR SOME COACHING

I've shown you the basics of "the model" and used it to show how we can see a couple of gospel principles with new eyes. I'll be doing more of that in the balance of the book.

But now I want to show you the power of the model in real lives. Its power becomes evident in the intimate coaching sessions I do with my clients as I help them discover the true source of their problems—their unconscious thoughts. So please put this book aside for a bit and witness these real-life coaching sessions, shared with the permission of actual clients. I think you'll find this "thought work" fascinating and really insightful. You'll be able to see yourself in these situations and begin to imagine the power of conscious thinking in your life.

Just scan the QR code provided on this page with the camera on your phone or on another device. If you are unable to watch now, make sure you return and catch it later. You won't be sorry you did.

https://jodymoore.com/bthbook/

For the earth is full, and there is
enough and to spare.

Doctrine and Covenants 104:17

04. THE LAW OF ABUNDANCE

Scarcity and Abundance

I have something important to tell you, and I hope you'll consider that I could be right about it. A part of your brain might be suspicious of the information I'm about to offer you, and there are good reasons for its skepticism. Your brain's primary function, which will override all other functions if necessary, is survival. More than anything, that amazing organ in your skull wants you and your offspring to live as long as possible. Your brain is constantly trying to prevent lack in your life so that the absence of something important won't kill you. It believes that if it can identify, predict, and fixate on all the ways that you or your life could be lacking, then it can head off disaster.

Thanks, brain.

And also . . . settle down.

This fixation on scarcity is left over from the days when humans lived in caves and might go days without food. Maybe our ancestors had to fight for the comfort and safety of a particular cave that was desirable to many. And maybe they had to rush to capture their dinner and get back to said cave before nightfall. Our ancestors needed this scarcity-driven brain to survive, and they have passed this trait down to us. But today? Today our challenges are different than the ones our primitive ancestors faced, and this scarce way of viewing ourselves and the world makes those challenges even more difficult to overcome.

Which brings me to the important thing I wanted to tell you.

I want you to know that there is more than enough.

Of everything.

Yes, really.

There is more than enough of everything you need and even more than enough of everything you want. I know it doesn't seem this way at times. Perhaps you feel like there isn't enough. I want to offer that this is not a reflection of the reality of your life; instead, your life is a reflection of the reality of your thoughts, whether those thoughts are based in scarcity or abundance.

Some individuals or groups of people in the world are at a great disadvantage relative to others. Some people have a lot, and others have barely enough to survive or not enough at times. I'm not suggesting we stop working to create more opportunities for underserved populations or even that we should all be content with where we are and not strive for more. I'm simply suggesting that no matter what our circumstances are, or what we are working to achieve in our own lives or in service to others, working from abundance is more beneficial than working from the easier feeling of scarcity.

If you've ever worried about not having a certain experience, not possessing enough time or money, or not getting enough done, you've experienced scarcity. If you feel behind in some way, or if you've made a purchase because you're afraid the item will sell out and you'll regret not buying it, or if you've lain in bed at night counting all the ways that *you* are not enough, then your thinking has been focused on scarcity. This type of thinking is not going to make you or your life better. We all experience scarcity thinking at times, but we can work to minimize it, and I highly recommend that you join me in doing so.

I realize that *abundance* and *scarcity* are buzzwords in the self-help world, and I'm sorry to play into the cliché of a life coach by using them. However, I have seen that when people shift their thoughts from scarcity to abundance they make some of the most powerful and exciting transformations ever. And I would be holding back if I didn't invite you to experiment with these ideas in your own life.

Let's look at a generic model that illustrates a problem caused by scarcity thinking and the change that can happen with a more abundant mindset:

Circumstance: I am selling a product.

Thought: If people don't buy this, I'm in trouble.

Feeling: Scarcity.

Action: Sell in a needy and desperate way that repels customers. Become discouraged. Hate making sales calls. Don't have much fun.

Result: I don't sell much, and I am "in trouble."

Here's an alternative model with a more consciously abundant thought:

Circumstance: I am selling a product.

Thought: There are plenty of people who want this, and I will find them.

Feeling: Abundance.

Action: I present the product with more confidence. I find creative ways to illustrate its value, and I keep going until I find the right customers. I enjoy the process more, learn from mistakes, and am motivated to keep trying new things.

Result: I sell more, helping my customers and myself.

Notice how our actions change when fueled by thoughts of abundance versus scarcity. In both models we are attempting to sell a product, but I'm sure you've been the customer on the other side. You can feel the difference between interacting with a salesperson who is operating from scarcity and one who is operating from abundance. One makes us skeptical while the other gets us excited to make the right purchase. We are in control of the results we create through our actions, and thoughts rooted in abundance are always the best fuel for those actions.

In any area in which we create scarcity, we can turn our thoughts around; the Lord knows this about us. He knows that if we can get our heads in a more abundant place, we will create more of what we want and need. He knows that when we believe in the abundance of this life we will benefit ourselves and the people we know, love, and serve, so He offers us many opportunities to think abundantly. One of my favorite examples of this is the law of tithing.

In 3 Nephi 28:10 we read, "Bring ye all the tithes into the storehouse, that there may be meat in my house; and prove me now herewith, saith the Lord of Hosts, if I will not open you the windows of heaven and pour you out a blessing that there shall not be room enough to receive it." I believe that the Lord asks us to pay a 10 percent tithe in part to help us foster an abundant mindset.

Have you ever heard a church talk or lesson that includes the story about the person whose car had broken down? The person didn't know how they were going to fix it or get to work, but they made the decision to pay their tithing anyway, and then a miracle occurred. The car just started working, a check showed up unexpectedly, or a friend with a reliable car got a job right next door to this person's workplace. I used to roll my eyes at these stories. Not because I thought these things were impossible, but because I thought stories like these were one of the reasons why religion gets misinterpreted as being for delusional people who just want to feel better.

Then something interesting happened when I became a coach and started learning from teachers, thinkers, and mindset experts who are not members of the Church. I started hearing similar unlikely, and therefore "magical-sounding," stories from nonreligious people. These stories sounded oddly like the ones I'd hear in a fast and testimony meeting at church. People would talk about how they simply believed that something would work out, and then it did—although often not in the way they had expected. The mindset experts I had been studying taught that believing things will turn out creates that result in the end.[1] I often ponder the law of tithing and wonder if the Lord, by asking us to give in this way, is trying to prepare us to receive all that we desire and need. He knows that if we freely give up something, believing that we will have everything we need (even if we aren't sure how), then we will be able to receive the things we need in our lives. The power of an abundant mindset is illustrated in 2 Corinthians 9:6: "But this I say, He which soweth sparingly shall reap also sparingly; and he which soweth bountifully shall reap also bountifully." Let's put this idea into a model.

Circumstance: Tithing.

Thought: I will pay this because I love the Lord and know I will always have exactly what I need.

Feeling: Abundance.

Action: I pay my tithing with love. I notice opportunities, create what I need, show up confidently, get resourceful, and become better at creating value in the world.

Result: I always have exactly what I need.

The Lord teaches that if we aren't keeping a commandment with a willing heart, or if we are seeking outside approval or other forms of reward, then we will lose the blessings we would have gained through keeping that commandment: "Take heed that ye do not your alms before men, to be seen of them: otherwise ye have no reward of your Father which is in heaven."[2] In other words, some of my *actions* (like paying tithing) might be the same, but the thought and feeling that are fueling the actions will determine where my heart is, which will affect the result in my life. Let's look at a different model about tithing:

> **Circumstance:** Tithing.
> **Thought:** This is going to make my budget tight.
> **Feeling:** Scarcity.
> **Action:** I pay my tithing begrudgingly or with worry. I lack confidence, and I don't see opportunities or have the motivation to pursue them. Everything feels hard and scary, and I am less likely to be effective or provide value.
> **Result:** I have a hard time making ends meet.

I'm not saying that paying tithing with a less-than-perfect attitude isn't a useful first step. Sometimes we must begin out of obedience. But an abundant mindset drives different actions and therefore creates a different result than a scarce mindset does.

As humans, we are in a state of expansion and growth. It is natural to want for more because the pursuit of more requires growth and evolution, and part of our earthly experience is to continuously become new versions of ourselves. But when I say *more*, I don't mean it in the way most people think of the word. A bigger house or faster car is often not the kind of desire that is expansive (although there can be great and expansive reasons for new cars and houses). But *more* in the form of material possessions is not what we *truly* desire. What we truly want is

THE LAW OF ABUNDANCE

to feel less ashamed, worried, inadequate, insecure, or afraid. These emotions are all based in lack or scarcity, and scarcity at its extreme feels like fear. What we truly want is to feel more happiness, love, joy, and peace. These emotions are abundant, and abundance at its strongest feels a lot like love.

Perhaps you are single and really want to get married. Ask yourself why. You might say that you want to start a family and that you want to experience what it's like to be a spouse. OK, but ask yourself why you want those things. If you keep asking why, you'll find that at the root of your desire to get married is either a desire to avoid feeling something negative like loneliness (lack/fear) or a desire to feel something positive like love and excitement (abundance/love).

Maybe you have a child who is on drugs and you desperately want that child to stop taking drugs. Why? Your first answer may be that you don't want your child to suffer the consequences of choosing drugs. There's nothing wrong with that, but again, why? Dig deep enough and you'll find that you want to feel less worried or anxious (lack/fear) and instead feel more peace (abundance/love).

Or maybe your life feels pretty smooth right now but you really want to lose those last ten pounds once and for all. Why do you want this? Because you believe you will feel more confident (abundance/love) on the other side of ten pounds.

So, as you can see, scarcity and abundance apply to more than surface-level things like possessions. We desire families, experiences, and relationships. We want to learn skills, develop talents, create, and achieve goals. We also desire to protect our loved ones and to help others. Abundance in all of these areas will serve us far better:

From desperation and loneliness, I'm not as excited about dating, which might make it harder to get married.

83

From panic and fear, I'm a less effective mother and less influential in my child's life.

From self-loathing, I gravitate toward the distraction of cookies and ice cream, which doesn't help me lose those ten pounds.

An abundant mindset includes knowing not only that there is enough money in the world but, more powerfully, that there is enough life to be lived and that each of us *is* enough. The effect of knowing these two truths runs deep within us; this is why, for so many people, the phrase "You are enough" hits home in such a powerful way. It's a simple and obvious statement, but its message is easier for most people to believe about others than about themselves.

If you want to cultivate more abundance in your life, you can start with an issue that many people's brains use to create scarcity: money. A woman I coached years ago told me that she never gets the things she wants. She watched her neighbors go on vacations and buy nice homes and clothing, but she said that she didn't have the money to do that. In response, I asked her to tell me about the things she already has, and she struggled to answer me. I could tell from her demeanor that this woman not only didn't consider what she already owned but didn't fully appreciate her own worth. She had trouble looking me in the eye. She doubted herself in many ways. I told her that she is feeling scarcity not because of the things she is unable to do or achieve but because she is unable to achieve what she desires while she's living in scarcity.

This coaching session took place online, so I pointed out to my client that she had an internet connection in her home. She also had a device with which to talk with me. As we spoke, I could see that she appeared to have electricity and that there was a nice bookcase full of books behind her. When I asked, she

admitted that she had running water in her house. As I continued to point out the abundance of her life she rolled her eyes,
indicating that none of these things seemed impressive enough
in her mind. But I encouraged her to, for a moment, be in awe
of the world she had created and stop looking to others for proof
that her life was enough.

Next, we explored her beliefs about her own worth, and
just as I had suspected, she struggled to see or acknowledge
it. She could not tell me with confidence anything that was
amazing about herself. I pointed out that she was on a call with
a life coach, which indicated she was open minded. She was
telling a stranger her fears, proving she was brave enough to
be vulnerable. I promised her that there is a never-ending list
of characteristics worth celebrating but that she needs to choose
to look for it. She is already complete; she doesn't need to do
or be or have anything more for that to be true. And ironically
enough, once she can allow herself to understand that truth
more fully, she will do and have and create more in her life.
But having more of what she wants won't create her feelings of
abundance or completeness—she'll already have those feelings
because she's chosen abundant thoughts about herself and her
life along the way.

All this is true for you too, my friend.

An abundant view of the world, your life, and yourself
will serve you far better than scarcity. And that view is entirely
available to you.

Because many of us have a scarcity mindset with money, I
love to practice generating abundance using the topic of money.
I have also had to work at creating abundance in this area, but
here are a few things I do deliberately that have worked for me.
Instead of being annoyed about paying the utility bill, I pay it

with gratitude that we have access to the convenience of modern utilities, and I remind myself that if our utilities were turned off I would beg the providers to take my money and turn them back on. Before I give money to a man on the side of the road holding a sign asking for help I take the money in my hands and silently say to it, "I don't know what he's going to do with you. He might not be a good steward of you. That part is not up to me. But thank you for being in my life for a while. I hope you can bless his life for good as well." And when I pay my tithing, I do so with tremendous gratitude to the Lord for the abundance of my life and this world. I acknowledge that everything surrounding me is His to begin with and that I am so happy to give a little bit back out of love and faith in His plan.

Abundance is simply the truth of what is. It's what Doctrine and Covenants 104:17 teaches when it says, "For the earth is full, and there is enough to spare; yea, I prepared all things, and have given unto the children of men to be agents unto themselves."

Did you hear that? Enough. And to spare. But you are the agent of what happens next.

––––––––––

1. See, for example, *The Power of Positive Thinking*, by Norman Vincent Peale, and *Think and Grow Rich*, by Napoleon Hill.
2. Matthew 6:1.

And whatsoever ye shall ask the
Father in my name, which is right,
believing that ye shall receive,
behold it shall be given unto you.

3 Nephi 18:20

05. PRAYER

The Eye Sees What the Mind Looks For

On the route between your home and someplace you regularly travel to, how many houses have a "For Sale" sign posted in front? My guess is that if you are a real estate agent or are looking to buy a house you might know the answer to that question; otherwise, you don't know at all. That's fascinating, don't you think? Every single day, you probably pass "For Sale" signs that you don't notice at all. This is because you brain deems the signs irrelevant, so you don't waste energy becoming aware of them. It's so efficient, that brain of yours.

Our brain truly is phenomenal. Stimulus (what we see, hear, taste, touch, or smell) comes in as information through the body, and the brain rapidly sifts through it and filters out anything that is not relevant.[1] We would be exhausted and ineffective if we took everything in. For example, pause for a moment and notice all the sounds you've blocked out to focus on reading this book. Is there a TV or music on in the distance? People having a conversation? How about the hum of a fan or heater? Is the refrigerator or dishwasher making a sound? Is there a clock ticking? There is more than you realized, right? Your brain knows that the sounds are not relevant to what you are doing, so it is blocking them out. And that's just auditory stimulus. If you stop reading for a moment and look around, you'll notice all the visual stimulus around you. Consider how much information our brain disregards as irrelevant in every moment in order to save our focus for what does matter.

Have you ever wondered why the people you live with can relax when the house is a mess and you cannot? I recently went to the basement to find my four kids playing video games. All eyes were glued to the screen and thumbs were moving ferociously over the controllers (why are controllers so complicated these days?). The kids were surrounded by toys, blankets, pillows, and empty water bottles, and an *entire* bag of popcorn was dumped upside down onto the carpet, and not one of them was the least bit bothered by this disaster scene.

Now, here's the interesting part: I know my kids, and they are not slobs. They don't like to get dirty; they prefer things to be simple and clean. But they are fine to sit and play video games in the midst of this mess because their brains can and will block it out. They don't notice the mess because they don't have thoughts that would make it relevant.

But not me.

I have many thoughts about that popcorn all over the floor.

My thoughts are about all the work this mess has created for me. They include opinions about kids and rules and disobedience. I start judging my children and feeling sorry for myself. And since I'm on the judgment train now, I'll throw in some judgment of myself for my inconsistency in enforcing rules and my failure to teach my kids how to clean up like successful humans should.

In other words, I make the circumstance of popcorn on the floor mean quite a few things, and this is the reason why I cannot sit and relax in the midst of it. But to my children the mess is much less relevant than whatever they are doing on that screen.

The eye sees what the mind looks for.

While it can be extremely useful in many cases, you should know that this brain feature can also be detrimental because the brain can't filter out information just because we say "don't see it." The eye sees whatever the mind looks for, whether it's something we want or don't want to see. If I tell you "Don't think of a yellow school bus," what just happened in your head? You thought of one, didn't you? Even though I told you not to, the brain hears only that yellow school buses are relevant. If I told you to make sure to not notice yellow school buses on the road all day today, you know what would happen, right? They'd begin jumping out at you everywhere because your brain is now focused on them. So while planning, being informed, and taking precautions to avoid problems can be useful to an extent, overly focusing on something we don't want is actually inviting more of that thing into our focus and therefore into our lives.

Race car drivers are taught that if their car begins to skid out of control they need to avoid looking at large objects that they don't want to crash into (think telephone poles, for example). Because even if a driver is looking at an object and thinking *Watch out for that telephone pole!* the brain only knows that now telephone poles are relevant, so the body will work together with the brain and the driver will become more likely to steer directly into the pole. Drivers instead learn to look in the direction of the road, the dirt, or someplace where they *want* the car to go.[2] Brains are amazing.

What does this have to do with prayer? I'll tell you.

Prayer is a version of conscious thinking because when we pray we intentionally direct our minds toward what we want to "say" to our Father in Heaven. Maybe you say your prayer out loud, maybe you whisper it, or maybe you say it in your head. Doesn't matter. When you pray, you are thinking thoughts and focusing your brain in a more meditative, receiving state. You're telling your brain what to focus on and learning to still your mind. What we focus on, we head toward, we create more of, and we attract into our lives. And the Lord answers.

There are many ways to say it, but the point is the same: we get what we seek if we seek it with belief. This is one reason, possibly, why consistent heartfelt prayer with our Heavenly Father serves us so well.

Does He really need us to tell Him what we're thinking? If He knows my heart and every hair on my head,[3] then He also knows my thoughts.[4] He doesn't really need me to tell Him.

I need to tell Him.

For my own benefit.

I need to direct my mind toward the things I want so that I can tell my brain what to look for and create in my life. Loving Heavenly Parents are always sending me what I need. But my brain may filter out these blessings as irrelevant if I'm not telling my brain that they *are* relevant. And prayer is an especially useful way to tell my brain what to look for.

Part of my coaching business model includes publishing a new podcast episode every week. The podcast serves several purposes: teaching my clients so that during coaching sessions I can spend more time coaching and less time teaching, putting thought-work tools into more hands, and helping people who are not yet clients know whether my program is the right fit for them. And I've been doing this for nearly six years.

Do you know what that means?

It means I've published more than three hundred podcast episodes on over three hundred different topics, and I don't see an end to this train because it's a fantastic ride and is serving so many people. It also means that topic ideas for future podcast episodes are particularly relevant to my brain. I even pray for guidance on which topics to discuss.

People ask me if I'm worried I'll run out of ideas, and I tell them not in the least. Because the podcast is so relevant to me, I find ideas for it everywhere. When I'm in line at the grocery store waiting to check out, I often overhear conversations. Sometimes it's someone having a heated argument on their cell phone, and other times it's two people discussing their thoughts about the headline of a magazine displayed by the checkout. To me these observations are full of potential podcast topics. I can be listening to another podcast, an audiobook, or even a Church talk on a subject that is in no way related to the work I do, and I'll open up the notes app on my phone and capture the idea it just gave me for a podcast episode. Sometimes even a seemingly everyday conversation with a friend gives me an idea for what to publish that week.

For example, I recently went on a walk with a friend who told me about a struggle she was having with family members who she felt didn't understand her. She felt they were judging her unfairly and was hurt when she thought about their disapproval. On the walk I stayed in friend mode (I don't coach my friends unless we are on an actual coaching call) and empathized with her, told her I think she's amazing, and validated her pain. But the conversation gave me the idea to create what has become one of my most-downloaded podcast episodes, "Allowing People to Be Wrong About You."

The eye sees what the mind looks for. It's brilliant.

Let's remember the way in which we are taught to pray.[5] After opening our prayer and addressing God, we converse with Him. We express gratitude for all the things we appreciate. Thanking Him is extremely useful because it directs our brain to the good things, and we get to feel gratitude, which we already know is valuable. With this practice, we invite into our lives more of the blessings for which we are grateful—more of what we already have and still want.

Next, we ask Him for what we need, again putting a focus on what we want to bring into our awareness or create for ourselves. As we speak with our Heavenly Father, we are literally telling our brains what to look for and create. And in a more open, meditative form of prayer, we can even take a step beyond what we think we need and want, and open ourselves up to what the Lord wants for us. Either way, we focus our minds in a useful way through prayer. Of course, this doesn't mean that we don't share our concerns or worries, but notice that when we pray there is a different approach than when we're just complaining.

When I want to complain, I like to call one of my sisters. They are both good at allowing me to vent, not trying to solve problems I don't really want to solve, and offering a little bit of validation or empathy. I hope you have someone like this in your life. Sometimes it helps to just say out loud what is bothering you. But when I am ready to improve things, change myself, or solve the problem, it's a different conversation. I might still call one of my sisters, but I'll say, "OK, I need ideas," or "What do you think about me trying this approach?"

When we pray, it is in the spirit of seeking, not in the spirit of complaining. For example, we don't say, "This part of my day was the *worst*, Heavenly Father. You wouldn't believe what a jerk the guy at the grocery store was." That's just not the spirit of prayer as I have come to understand it. It might be, "Please help me to be more patient with people like the man I encountered today." Our thoughts are focused on how we can gain patience, which is a pretty useful thing for our brains to go to work on. When we tell our brains what problems we'd like to solve, we begin noticing all the ways in which we can solve those problems. This process is so powerful that it can feel a bit like magic. I know this because I have felt it working during some of the challenges I've experienced.

I have stomach problems. I'm not sure why, but my dad has the same issues, as do many of my siblings. We've all been tested for everything under the sun and have tried everybody's recommendations to relieve the symptoms. As far as I can tell, my stomach pain flares up most when I'm eating too much junk food, when I am stressed, or when there seems to be no reason at all. I've learned to manage it for the most part by watching my diet, staying hydrated, and taking pain medication when necessary. However, when I'm pregnant the problem seems to be more intense and less preventable, and I am unable to take my go-to pain medication.

When I was pregnant with my third child, my stomach pain was especially bad. I couldn't sleep or find any relief. My husband gave me a blessing, and I was praying fervently. I prayed to find a remedy that would be safe for my baby and would provide some comfort. Praying was one way for me to tell my brain that finding a solution to this stomach problem was relevant and that it needed to filter out unnecessary things until we solved the problem.

One day, I had a routine prenatal check-up at the doctor's office, where I knew all the nurses and had visited many times before. This appointment was different, though. A nurse I had never seen before helped me. I can't remember her explanation for being there that day, but I didn't think much of it until I began talking with her and she asked how I was feeling. I told her about my stomach pain, and while most physicians and nurses dismissed it, she was curious. She asked me multiple questions and then told me that she had similar symptoms. She suggested that I try sleeping in more of a sitting-up position, propped up on as many pillows as I could be comfortable on. She believed that if I did this, my symptoms would lessen.

It sounded too easy to be useful.

I was skeptical that it would help.

I was also desperate for relief, so I did as she instructed. The next morning I woke up with almost no pain in my stomach. I was in complete awe. I called my siblings, and they reacted to the nurse's suggestion with the same optimistic skepticism I had but agreed to test it out. Amazingly, we've all found at least some relief with this method. I never saw that nurse again— not through the rest of that pregnancy nor during the one I would have a couple of years later. I tell people all the time that the nurse was an angel who came to help me in answer to my prayers, and she is. Maybe she's an angel living as a person on earth, but to me she is an angel nonetheless.

I am so grateful that Heavenly Father is there and listening to me. When I ask Him for what I need, He directs me toward it. He puts events and people who can help me in my path, and He gave me a brain that works to identify them. When I tell my brain to focus on solutions, it is capable of doing so in amazing ways. Perhaps if I hadn't been focused on finding a solution to my stomachaches, I wouldn't have brought the subject up with the nurse. After all, when she asked how I was feeling, she was asking specifically about the pregnancy. But, thanks to the prayer

I had said earlier, my brain was focused on finding a treatment that wouldn't harm my baby. Perhaps Heavenly Father wouldn't have put her in my path otherwise. Who knows. What I do believe is that when we focus on what we appreciate, what we need, or what we want, we invite those things into our lives—and prayer is one of the most powerful tools we can use to accomplish this.

I know that life is much more complicated than this story. The Lord doesn't always answer our prayers the way we'd like Him to. Sometimes His timing is different than ours, or we feel that we aren't receiving answers at all. But I do believe that Heavenly Father gave each of us a brain and that a part of it is designed to help us seek out the things we want and need. Prayer is one way we can keep our focus on things that will serve us.

Here is the model I used to help me through my stomachache issues. You could replace the circumstance line with a challenge you are facing and try it out for yourself.

Circumstance: I'm having stomach pain during my pregnancy.

Thought: I know I can ask the Lord to help me figure this out.

Feeling: Curious and hopeful.

Action: I pray to ask for help and then I speak with people who I think might have solutions.

Result: I am open to noticing the solutions that the Lord helps provide.

The Power of Stillness

We live in a hectic world. Everyone everywhere wants a piece of our time, our money, and our attention, and I don't know about you, but I'm often happy to give it away.

I like TV.

I love my phone.

I enjoy scrolling Pinterest and Instagram and watching makeup tutorials on YouTube, only to keep doing my makeup the exact same way I have for the last twenty-five years.

It's fun, this world we live in. Thanks to the internet, we have endless access to things we can watch or purchase. We can watch TV without commercials, and we don't even have to wait for the right day or time for a favorite show to come on. We just click, search, and *boom*. The show is ready to watch. What a world.

Some of the noise in our world is junk, but many of our distractions are grounded in goodness. I like listening to audiobooks as I tidy up the house or to a podcast while I'm getting ready in the morning. The amount of knowledge available and the ease with which we can access it is truly incredible, and I am grateful to be alive to experience it. Sometimes I wonder, however, if amid all of this stimulus we are losing the ability to be still.

Stillness matters.

There is power in taking time to be quiet, to listen to our thoughts, and to connect with the Divine and hear inspiration, revelation, and wisdom. But when our brain is not used to stillness, it may find the quiet extremely uncomfortable, and we may feel fearful or anxious as a result. The brain does not prefer a blank slate on which to draw anything; it prefers stimulus—something external it can latch on to and think about.

Many of today's experts in neuroscience and psychology find meditation to be beneficial.[6] There are a variety of meditation methods, and I won't get into them here because I am not an expert in this area, but essentially, to meditate is to practice directing one's mind. It's developing the ability to direct the brain toward stillness and away from the busyness of our thoughts. It's dropping into what is true and real, which is always peaceful and centering. Meditation helps us find truth, which can be hard to find underneath all of our brain chatter.

Truth feels steady, calm, and loving. Truth is what we know intrinsically and what the Spirit confirms for us. And then there are all the thoughts our brains lay on top of truth. That's what I call brain chatter. What I love about the practice of prayer, when I do it sincerely, is that it helps me be still and find truth. Prayer is the practice of quieting my brain chatter and connecting with the Divine, where all truth resides. It is the practice of not listening to my thoughts but instead talking to the source of all peace and love, who is God.

Stillness matters.

Back when I was still working in a corporate career and living in California, I found myself questioning whether I was doing the right thing by continuing to work full-time after I had children. The high heels and paychecks were fun but not as important to me as being there for my kids or following the path the Lord wanted for me. But I was afraid to get still and hear Him because I didn't want Him to tell me to quit my job. Instead, I kept so busy with that job and those kids that I couldn't really hear much above all the noise of the world and in my head. And this worked.

Sometimes.

However, the thought that I should bring this question to the Lord was always nagging at me. At that time my husband was making enough money to support us. My children were ages two and three, and every day I had to commute in Southern California traffic to take them to Polly's house (who watched them while I worked) and then get myself to and from work. We spent more time on the 605 freeway than we did in our own backyard.

This was my life until one morning when I finally got still. It was raining as I loaded the kids into the car and then turned the heater on. Now that I was acclimated to Southern California, a little rain felt like a winter day to me, and I was freezing. Besides, some heat often helped the little ones fall asleep on the drive, making it easier on all of us.

If you've lived in a place that gets winter snow, then you would be confused by Southern California drivers in the rain. Light rain does not really make for hazardous road conditions, other than limiting your visibility a bit. But nobody in Southern California seems to know this, and when it rains everyone drives at a slow, creeping pace, as you would on icy roads. So on this particular morning our long commute became even longer. While creeping along the freeway with a little heat on my feet, two sleeping angels in the back seat, and rain lightly tapping on my roof, I considered whether I should call a friend, listen to my audiobook, or put on music. Then I had the thought to just be still. I brushed it away at first, still sifting through the options in my head, but I finally decided that the pitter patter of rain was enough to keep me company, and I began reflecting on my life.

I thought about how much I loved my kids and wondered if dragging them all over the freeways of California every day was too much. I wondered if we would be OK if we tried living on just my husband's salary. I mostly wondered if I would be OK if I quit work and stayed at home with the kids. I felt scared just imagining it. The fear was immediately followed by guilt. Was I being selfish? What was wrong with me? Why did all the other women in my ward love being at home with their kids and I didn't? Was I making a mistake?

As I continued to be in the stillness of this question, my mind shifted away from fear or guilt, and I felt overwhelmed with gratitude. Gratitude for those kids and my husband. Gratitude for Polly for loving my children. Gratitude for that moment on the freeway where the world outside was busy but inside my car was stillness and warmth. But I also felt gratitude for my job and my company. It wasn't a formal prayer, but it was reverent and I felt the Spirit there as my heart filled with love thinking about all the people I had come to know at my job, the good work we were doing, and the things I was learning by being there.

And that's when I noticed the rainbow.

It was beautiful, as rainbows always are. The sun was shining through the clouds, and light rain was still coming down. But to me the most amazing part was that I could see the *entire* rainbow. It began on one side of the 605 freeway and ended on the other side. It made an arch right over the freeway, and we were about to drive directly underneath that rainbow. It was as though the rainbow was put there like a red carpet to tell us we were special. To tell us that we were going the right way. The rainbow arch was the way to Polly's house and to my job, and I felt the truth right then as the sight of that rainbow cleared away the brain chatter. The truth was that right then my job was a good thing for me and my family. The truth was that this might not always be the case, but right then I didn't have to make forever decisions about whether to work or stay at home. The truth was that it was OK for me to love going to work and that my children were in the best of hands with Polly, who loved them. The truth was that I am not like most of the other women I knew, and that was not a bad thing. The truth was that at this point the Lord wanted me to do what I wanted to do. I'm not suggesting that the rainbow was a sign from God or that answers will be as obvious in most cases, but sometimes something simple like nature combined with our willingness to be still can open us up to personal revelation and inspiration that we otherwise might miss.

Stillness and truth finding is something I am able to do well only on occasion. The great ones, the people who leave a legacy behind, they must get good at doing it frequently and doing it even in the most challenging of circumstances.

I recently heard a story about Dr. Martin Luther King Jr. and the famous speech he gave at the pinnacle of the civil rights movement. According to the story, Dr. King was supposed to deliver a different speech in Washington, DC, that day. His advisors had put a good deal of time and care into writing it for him. Dr. King began giving the prepared speech but knew it wasn't landing with the crowd. It was not moving people the way he had intended. It was falling flat. Part way into his speech he paused just long enough for a woman in the crowd to call out. She said, "Tell them about the dream!"

Dr. King abandoned the previously prepared speech. He got still, even in the midst of the 250,000 people gathered between the Lincoln Memorial and the Washington Monument. He accessed the truth and wisdom that resided within him and delivered what we know today as the "I Have a Dream" speech. And what lived within him was more powerful than anything anyone else could have told him to say.[7]

John 14:27 reads, "Peace I leave with you, my peace I give unto you: not as the world giveth, give I unto you. Let not your heart be troubled neither let it be afraid." This unique peace is available to us only through Christ, and how will we access it if we don't get still enough to feel His influence? I've never been good at sitting on the ground with my legs folded, my hands on my knees, and my mind focused on my breath. If you are able to do that, I respect you. I am up for the challenge of learning to be that still—I don't doubt the power of it. But prayer (formal or informal), meditation, and stillness are things that I believe our heads and hearts crave. I believe they are where we access truth. We have amazing wisdom within us, but to take full advantage of that wisdom we must first choose to listen. We can connect with ourselves in the stillness, and we can hear the Spirit there. Choose any method you want, but please, my friend, be still.

---

1. Jordan Gaines Lewis, "This Is How the Brain Filters Out Unimportant Details," *Psychology Today*, February 11, 2015, https://www.psychologytoday.com/us/blog/brain-babble/201502/is-how-the-brain-filters-out-unimportant-details.

2. Harrison Barnes, "Ferraris Crashing into Poles and the Importance of Focus in Your Life and Career," *HarrisonBarnes.com*, March, 18 2015, https://www.harrisonbarnes.com/ferraris-crashing-into-poles-and-the-importance-of-focus-in-your-life-and-career/.

3. Matthew 10:30.

4. Doctrine and Covenants 6:16.

5. "How to Pray," *Come Unto Christ*, accessed April 30, 2021, https://www.comeuntochrist.org/beliefs/prayer/how-to-pray.

6. Matthew Thorpe, "12 Science-Based Benefits of Meditation," *Healthline*, July 5, 2017, https://www.healthline.com/nutrition/12-benefits-of-meditation.

7. Jon Meacham, "MLK Jr., The Last Speech," September 2, 2020, episode 1, in It Was Said, produced by C13Originals Studios, podcast, 44:00, https://podcasts.apple.com/us/podcast/ep-1-mlk-jr-the-last-speech/id1527280716?i=1000489821686.

I, the Lord, will forgive whom I will
forgive, but of you it is required
to forgive all men.

Doctrine and Covenants 64:10

06. FORGIVENESS

What Would Love Do?

As members of the Church, we understand well that we've been commanded to forgive others repeatedly. Even when they don't deserve it. Even when they aren't sorry. We've been taught to forgive over and over and over again if necessary.[1] I've noticed that during church lessons on forgiveness we all seem to understand that this is what the Lord did so well, and we seem to be on board with forgiving. We even agree that feeling vengeful and angry only punishes us because those emotions feel awful. In theory, forgiveness is a no-brainer.

But on the other side of theory is the real-life human brain.

At times, the real-life human brain has a hard time forgiving. Because, maybe you've noticed, people do some pretty terrible things. People lie and cheat and steal and judge and abuse and harm and . . . I don't really need to explain this to you. It's impossible not to hear about all the awful things happening in the world, and it's impossible to escape this life without some of the people in it behaving badly toward us or the people we love. There goes our friend agency again, keeping things interesting.

So, how do we forgive someone who has broken our trust, broken a commandment, or broken the law? What if most people would agree that this person can't be trusted? What if the person isn't even sorry and we need to set a boundary or protect ourselves or others from this potentially dangerous person? The answer to these questions begins with another useful question:

What would love do?

Melissa, one of my clients who is an active member of the Church, told me that her father, also a member of the Church, had used the gospel to shame and judge her as she was growing up. He had also physically and sexually abused her and her sisters and told Melissa that she was worthless and that no man would want to marry her.

He was wrong.

In many ways.

Today Melissa is married to a wonderful man and has two young children of her own. She has wrestled with her testimony and now has a strong one; she finds peace in her knowledge of the gospel. She even wants to forgive her father. For a long time, Church leaders have advised her to forgive him and have told her that her father wants to be a part of her life. Melissa told me that she doesn't want to leave her kids with this man because she's afraid he may harm them. "How can I forgive him?" she asked me. I replied that we would get to that question, but first we must ask, "What would love do?"

When we ponder this question, we must apply it to everyone in the story. In my client's story, we have Melissa, her children, and her father. Love is considering everyone involved; when we operate from love, we are acting as the Savior does. Love doesn't give everyone what they want all the time. Sometimes love says no. Sometimes love sets boundaries. But love doesn't do these things to be vengeful. It does so out of, well, love.

In this scenario, love says, "I love you Dad, and I'm not comfortable leaving my kids alone with you." Love doesn't hold on to anger about what happened in the past, but it doesn't allow more harm and danger in the present or future, if possible. Love is wise and kind, but it is strong and confident. Above all, love tells the truth. Love says, "Sometimes I still feel hurt when I think about what happened in the past," but love also says, "I want to let it go."

Forgiveness is not something you do. It's something that happens internally because it comes from your thoughts. Forgiveness is a belief system that creates a feeling of love, or at least compassion or curiosity. However, trying to love someone who you believe has wronged you in some way will be challenging if you aren't loving yourself first. Remember, when you choose love, you choose it for everyone involved. The person who wronged you is still worthy of love no matter what. But so are you, as you've always been, and that is the part most people skip over when they are in the process of forgiving.

How to Let It Go

I'm as sick of the song "Let It Go" as you are, but there's a reason it caught on, and it wasn't just Elsa's flowing white hair, magical voice, and gigantic eyes. The message is spot-on. There is so much peace available when we finally just "let it go." It's a huge relief.

The relief of letting go reminds me of the days when I had to lug an infant carrier around. You know, the seat that so conveniently clips in and out of the base buckled down in the car?

While I drove, the baby was safely strapped in, and when I got to church, to the grocery store, or to Target, I just unlocked the seat from its base and took it with me. Hopefully at this point my baby was asleep and would stay asleep while she stayed cozy in the carrier. What a world. The only problem is those carriers are big, heavy, and awkward.

To free up both of my hands, I used to try looping the handle over my forearm, like a fashionable handbag that was neither fashionable nor a handbag. This was not a good idea because at one point I developed bruises on both forearms. I was never fit enough to be carrying that much weight around, due to the havoc wreaked on my body from growing a baby, giving birth to a baby, and feeding a baby. All with my body.

My point is that, after my errands were done, it always felt amazing to set that infant carrier down and hear it click into its little home base in the car. The baby was safe and I was free from the weight.

This is the kind of relief we feel when we forgive. We carry around a weight when we hold on to anger. We create pain and suffering for ourselves when we resent and fume and ruminate. Elder Kevin R. Duncan of the Seventy said, "Even though we may be a victim once, we need not be a victim twice by carrying the burden of hate, bitterness, pain, resentment, or even revenge. We can forgive and we can be free!"[2]

Holding on to anger punishes us, and only us, because we have to feel those terrible feelings when we create them for ourselves. The people we are mad at don't feel them. They might feel something negative, but only if they create negativity for themselves with their own thoughts. So the idea that we are somehow letting perpetrators off the hook if we forgive them is ridiculous. When we carry around anger and resentment, we punish ourselves for other people's bad behavior. A part of us thinks that maybe holding on to a grudge will change others, but in reality, it changes only us. And not in a good way. Let it go. That's what Melissa wanted to do. She was tired of carrying the weight around.

I believe that the commandment to forgive is not to benefit others; it's to benefit us. We are told to forgive, not because it's the "nice" thing to do or even because it's what we "should" do, but because of how much better we will feel and how amazing we can make our lives when we let go of that heavy carrier full of anger, resentment, bitterness, and fear. These emotions do not make for a cute baby. They are not useful, and we truly can let them go if we want to.

The way to do that is both simple and difficult.

It's to change your thinking.

The way we think about other people, specifically about their behavior in this case, creates our emotions about them. In addition, the way we think about ourselves in relation to other people creates emotions that we also must examine to let them go. To illustrate this principle, I want to break forgiveness down into two phases.

Phase One

The first phase of forgiveness is gaining awareness of your thoughts. This is important. Many of my clients want to skip this step so they can get straight to forgiving and letting go of bitterness. While I'm glad they have the desire to do this, it's challenging for them to do without first acknowledging and embracing their current thoughts. Imagine that you want to get directions from your GPS. You can type in where you want to go, but then the GPS system needs to identify where you are currently. That is the only way it can calculate the route properly. This idea applies to changing your thinking.

Acknowledging what you're currently thinking (even if your thoughts are mean, childish, and even illogical) is necessary to get started on the path toward the thoughts you want to have.

Recall a time you believed someone hurt you. How would you describe what happened? Take an honest, unedited look at what you're believing without judging your thoughts. The bitterness and anger you feel is real, so let's be honest about the thoughts creating these feelings. Pretending we don't have these thoughts doesn't get rid of them; it only sends them back into hiding. We must create a safe place to examine them if we are going to get leverage over them. Maybe you have thoughts like the following:

She knows better.
It's not fair.
I would never do that to him.
I can't believe he said that.
This is upsetting.
People shouldn't do that.
She is selfish.
He is difficult.

Perhaps your thoughts are more interesting or more dramatic than these, but when we are unable to forgive, it's usually because a version of one of these thoughts is keeping us stuck. Melissa and I did a brainstorm of all the thoughts she had about her dad, and it was challenging for her. She had pushed these thoughts down and had been telling herself to forgive and let it go for so long that she wasn't conscious of many of them anymore. But I assured her that her thoughts are valid and that observing them doesn't mean she has to keep them, and so we were able to find some. We chose a powerful thought and put it into a model to see what it was creating for her.

Circumstance: As a child I was abused by my father.

Thought: Many parts of my life have been harder as a result.

Feeling: Angry.

Action: Ruminate on the unfairness of it. Spin in self-pity. Compare my life to the lives of others. Resent people who seem to have it easier. Lack confidence as I pursue my goals.

Result: I continue to create pain and limit myself, making my life harder.

When Melissa discovered that this thought had been driving her for so long, she initially felt discouraged. But what I suggested to her, and would suggest to you if you can relate to Melissa's situation, is that she choose to feel compassion for herself instead. I explained that she was not wrong to be thinking this thought or creating this result. It was highly understandable. But now that she could see the result she'd created with this thought, she got to be the one in the power seat of her life.

I taught Melissa that while her father had power over her when she was a child, he didn't have that power anymore. But she continued to give him a kind of power by holding on to pain, and to let go of that pain didn't require her to believe that what he did was OK. If she wanted to, she could take all of the power back by changing the way she thinks about herself, her father, and her past. And this brings us to phase two.

Phase Two

In phase two of forgiveness, you choose a new thought to replace the old thought; however, I recommend that you take your time and that you observe yourself in your phase one model for as long as necessary. Don't rush or push the new thought/model on yourself because it likely won't stick. The brain is complicated. If you've been thinking the old thought for a long time, then your brain wants to keep thinking it. It's good at thinking it. It has gathered heaps of proof for that thought. So be delicate with your amazing brain, but be open to finding a new thought or even to being wrong about the current thought.

You may not realize this, but sometimes being wrong is the best thing ever. In fact, I'm always working to be better at it. Once I finally get my ego to settle down and I'm willing to be wrong about a thought that isn't serving me, I am open to believing a new thought. Sometimes, I can do a complete 180 in my thinking. Other times, I decide that I want to be right about the original thought but find a new direction to work toward. It's a slight change of trajectory, but the shift will still send me to a new location. You can do this too, my friend. And the great news is that the Lord will help you. He can help you find new thoughts, and He can help you loosen your grip on the old ones. And sometimes He can even help you love a person you never thought you could. Elder Kevin R. Duncan said, "At times, God may part the curtain and bless us with the gift to see into the heart, soul, and spirit of another person who has offended us. This insight may even lead to an overwhelming love for that person."[3]

Melissa and I took some time to consider what she wanted to think and feel. She wanted to keep believing that the way she was mistreated was terrible, and I wouldn't want her to believe anything otherwise. But we explored other thoughts that might be options for her. Because many different thoughts could be true in her situation.

For example, she is not broken. She is not any less capable of greatness than she might have been otherwise. She is a daughter of God and is loved beyond measure. She is, in fact, strong in ways she wouldn't have been without her struggle. And it's even possible that her life was always going to be hard. If she hadn't suffered abuse by her father, perhaps she would have had a different challenge, but her life was always going to be difficult. Maybe she's experiencing these challenges because she is so amazing that her life experience needed to be an honors-level class to help her become who God knows she could become. Maybe. Just maybe.

Now, you might be rejecting some of these thoughts. That's OK. I'm not suggesting that any of this is doctrine or that these thoughts are "truths." It's OK if you completely disagree with some of them. Trying on new thoughts is like trying on a new shade of lipstick. We all have different tastes, and what works for some doesn't work for others. My job was to open Melissa's mind up to the idea that she is allowed to think and believe *any thoughts* she wants to.

Really.

Anything.

We try thoughts on by first deciding whether we believe the thought, at least to a degree. If we do, we put the thought in a model to find out if it creates the feelings we want to feel and if those feelings drive the actions and results we want. Melissa wasn't ready for a 180-degree thought change such as, "My life was not any harder as a result." That's OK. She did find that a trajectory shift was powerful for her. The model she found and wanted to live from was the following:

Circumstance: As a child I was abused by my father.

Thought: My life was harder as a result *and that's OK*.

Feeling: Confident.

Action: I notice that I am OK. I focus on my life today and what I want for the future instead of living in the past. I notice strengths I have gained from of the challenges I've overcome. I push myself to set and achieve goals and stop telling myself I can't do it.

Result: I feel empowered and am pursuing the things I desire in my life.

I know these models are about Melissa and not about her father, who is the one she wants to forgive. At some point, she might have more thought-work to do on him, but she also might not. She might find that as she becomes more confident and empowered in her life that her head and her heart loosen their grip on the anger. That's what a trajectory change often does for people. If her new model doesn't end up working for her, we can do more models, but I wanted her to work on this one first because it takes time and practice to believe a new thought. Remember, the brain wants to keep thinking the thought it's already good at thinking. But if you gently redirect yourself to the new one, ask the Lord for help, and are willing for the process to take some time and practice, you really can rewire your brain to live from any thought that serves you.

Melissa's willingness to begin letting go of the past to make room in her life for new thoughts and goals beautifully illustrates a description of forgiveness that Elder James E. Faust referenced in a general conference talk: "Forgiveness is freeing up and putting to better use the energy once consumed by holding grudges, harboring resentments, and nursing unhealed wounds. It is rediscovering the strengths we always had and relocating our limitless capacity to understand and accept other people and ourselves."[4]

One of my favorite talks of all time was given by Michael Wilcox at Education Week in 2005. The talk is titled "When My Prayers Feel Unanswered," and in it he shares the following story. When Brother Wilcox was a young boy, his father left him, his brother, and his mother. His father had decided that he didn't want to be involved with the family, so his mother was left to raise two boys on her own. For many years Brother Wilcox struggled with pain over his father's decision, as anyone probably would, but when he was a young man he decided that he wanted to forgive his father. He began praying, asking the Lord to help him forgive, but he was unable to feel forgiveness.

When he got older, Brother Wilcox served a mission. He prayed many times before, during, and after his mission to be able to forgive, but he was again unable to let go of the pain. He eventually married in the temple, with still no success in forgiving his father. Years later, with a family of his own, Brother Wilcox found himself at home one afternoon preparing a sacrament meeting talk about families as his two boys played nearby. As he considered what he would say, he felt the Spirit prompt him to talk about his father. He was confused by this prompting because he didn't have any inspiring stories or happy memories to share about his father. In fact, he was still harboring ill feelings toward him. He felt that because his father was not around while he was growing up, his father had missed out on so many things. For illustration purposes, I've taken the liberty to put his story into a simple model:

> **Circumstance:** My father did not live with us while I was grow-ing up.
> **Thought:** I suffered tremendously because of this.
> **Feeling:** Angry.
> **Action:** Harbor pain. Try to let it go without success.
> **Result:** I continue to suffer.

Brother Wilcox lives his life close to the Spirit, so when he felt a prompting to think about his father, he was open. Being open is critical when you are trying to change your thinking. As Brother Wilcox continued watching his boys play, he reflected on all the precious memories he had with them, such as birthday parties, first days of school, and learning to ride bikes. He felt a tremendous love for his boys and gratitude for the experience of being their father. Then the Lord offered him a new thought: "Now that you are a father, now that you know a father's love and a father's joy, would you be the son who lost his father, or the father who lost his son?"[5]

Brother Wilcox sobbed when this thought entered his mind. As he took his two sons in his arms and hugged them, he cried not for himself but for his father. He realized in this moment that as much as he had suffered, his father had suffered even more as a result of his own decisions. Brother Wilcox didn't have to practice the new thought; it was powerful enough that he embraced it and was overcome with the emotions of it immediately.[6]

> **Circumstance:** My father did not live with us while I was growing up.
> **Thought:** My father missed out on one of the greatest joys of life: raising his sons.
> **Feeling:** Compassion and heartbreak.
> **Action:** Cry. Cherish the time I have with my sons. Forgive my father. Find relief from my anger.
> **Result:** I feel more love and empathy, which makes me a more whole person, a better father, and a better son.

Notice that in both models there is some "negative" emotion. Anger doesn't feel good, but neither does heartbreak. I believe that when people mistreat us or let us down we are going to want to feel something negative. But in the first model is the kind of pain that keeps you stuck. Experts in the field of psychology call this *dirty pain*.[7] Dirty pain is not useful. It doesn't help you heal from an experience. In the second model is a different kind of pain; we'll call it *clean pain*. Sadness or heartbreak can be cleansing, and I believe that clean pain refines us and helps us become more like God. We might not describe it as feeling good, but to me it feels like being alive.

David O. McKay explained that growing and evolving is why we have the gospel of Jesus Christ: "The purpose of the gospel is . . . to make bad men good and good men better, and to change human nature."[8] I believe that the process of moving through the painful parts of life, understanding that we create the pain with our thinking but accepting that we will want or need to at times, is a powerful part of this change that God desires for us.

Whenever you want to believe a new thought or live from a different model, turn to the Lord for help with your thought-work. He will whisper to you through the Spirit and will help to change your heart. He can also carry you through the pain that might be necessary to move forward. He designed our bodies to manage emotions—even the painful ones. And when you open up to these emotions and loosen your grip on the thoughts that aren't serving you, you will be amazed at what's possible, my friend. Let it go.

————————

1. Matthew 18:21–35.

2. Kevin R. Duncan, "The Healing Ointment of Forgiveness," *Ensign*, April 2016, https://www.churchofjesuschrist.org/study/general-conference/2016/04/the-healing-ointment-of-forgiveness?lang=eng.

3. Duncan, "Healing Ointment."

4. Sidney B. Simon and Suzanne Simon, *Forgiveness: How to Make Peace with Your Past and Get On with Your Life* (New York: Grand Central, 1991), 19, quoted in James E. Faust, "The Healing Power of Forgiveness," *Ensign*, May 2007, 68, https://www.churchofjesuschrist.org/study/general-conference/2007/04/the-healing-power-of-forgiveness?lang=eng.

5. S. Michael Wilcox, "When My Prayers Feel Unanswered" (talk, BYU Campus Education Week, August 2005), https://www.youtube.com/watch?v=yJSbnKli_04&index=7&list=PLP6OPpIXTS-RxCE8nIrSoW1iR4Sy_7LsC.

6. Wilcox, "When My Prayers Feel Unanswered."

7. Martha Beck, "Victory by Surrender," *Martha's Blog*, accessed September 19, 2020, https://marthabeck.com/2011/09/victory-by-surrender/.

8. From the film *Every Member a Missionary*, as acknowledged by Franklin D. Richards, CR, October 1965, 136–37; see also Brigham Young, JD 8:130 [22 July 1860].

And when we obtain any blessing
from God, it is by obedience
to that law upon which
it is predicated.

Doctrine and Covenants 130:21

07. OBEDIENCE

Don't tell me what to do.
You're not the boss of me.

I'll do what I want to, and you can't stop me.

You might think these are things my kids say to me, but actually my kids are more mature than that. I'm convinced that in the premortal world they were the adults, and when I was told I would get to be a mother I knew I would be a mess, so they said, "Don't worry. We'll be your kids. We can take it, and we'll take care of you."

The thoughts listed above are sentences that run through *my own* head with greater frequency than I care to admit. I once took Gretchen Rubin's Four Tendencies quiz to identify my account-ability type, and I fell into the Rebel category.[1] According to Gretchen Rubin, this isn't a cool James Dean sort of thing. Peo-ple with the Rebel tendency don't respond well to external or internal accountability, and when they feel they're being told what to do will often choose to do the opposite. I like to believe that my inclination to be a rebel is just an expression and defense of my agency. But in reality, it is immature and problematic that

I struggle to do what wise people advise me to do. Or at least sometimes this is true.

But then, there are other times.

There are situations in which I will take someone's advice and run with it.

I realized this as I've built my coaching practice over the past seven years. I became an entrepreneur out of necessity. Not the necessity of taking care of my finances. Not even the necessity of being able to work from home. The necessity of being a coach. When I discovered coaching, applied it to my life, and then learned how to use it to help others, I knew I had to do this work. I had to do it the same way that a shark has to keep moving or else it will die. I was a coach, and so I had to help people, and the only option I could find for doing so was to start my own business. I don't know if you've checked out Indeed or ZipRecruiter lately, but I have yet to see a job posting for a life coach. I was going to have to start from scratch, and even though I never desired to be an entrepreneur, I was willing to become one if it meant that I could also be a coach.

So I did.

But it wasn't as simple as that.

As the saying goes, I'm no rocket scientist. But the subject I possibly knew less about than rocket science was online business. I knew a little bit about sales, thanks to my corporate experience. I knew how to use my MacBook Pro to send emails to friends and family. I knew how to use Google and YouTube to "search it up," as my kids say when they need to understand something. Aside from that, I didn't even know what I didn't know. But luckily, I didn't need to, because there were (and still are) a slew of whip-smart individuals who had figured out the world of online business and wanted to teach it to me. People like Amy Porterfield, James Wedmore, and Russell Brunson started showing up in my social media newsfeed, offering me strategies for building and growing a business. Some people are skeptical about the way the internet tracks our searches and uses it to advertise to us. I personally love it. I like having the things I want and need right in front of me, and at this point in my life, what I wanted and needed were entrepreneurial strategies.

I began listening to individuals who had achieved what I wanted to achieve, I adapted their advice to my own style, and I did what they told me to do. I continued to learn from Brooke Castillo, who is not only an amazing coach but a brilliant entrepreneur, and I followed the strategies she suggested. That's it. I didn't push back and rebel against the advice I had received. I didn't have a toddler tantrum about not wanting to be told what to do. I actually really wanted these experts to tell me what to do because I trusted them. I knew that they knew better than I did how to get to where I wanted to go.

To be fair, just because I followed their advice doesn't mean that my business plans always worked the way I wanted them to. I had plenty of failures and setbacks along the way. But I continued to learn from and then follow the advice of successful entrepreneurs, and as a result I created the coaching practice I have today.

One day I visited a class of coaches in training at the Life Coach School, and they asked me to tell them why I was having so much success in my business. The truth is that, just like in any other industry, the number of people who desire to be successful in their entrepreneurial efforts as coaches compared to the number who actually achieve their goals is pretty dismal. "So why," these new coaches asked me, "have you been able to succeed, and how can we do the same?"

Here is what I told them, which is the honest truth: It's not that I am special in some way. It's not that I picked the right target market. It's not about my timing or about good luck or because I am secretly a unicorn. I simply followed the strategies I was taught. I did what I was told. I didn't question it or argue with it. I completed one step right after the other, believing that what I was doing would work and being willing to finesse the nuances of what I was taught to make it work for me, and it did work. To those aspiring entrepreneurs, I said, "Just do what your mentors tell you to do. Don't question it, even though you'll want to. You'll think it's too hard, it doesn't apply to you, it won't work for you, or you just don't want to do it. You'll think that you or your business are different in some way and so maybe you shouldn't follow your mentors' advice. Ignore your brain. Do it anyway." They thanked me for the advice, and I went on my way.

A few days after my visit to that coach training class I was driving home to my husband and kiddos and stopped to grab a few things at the grocery store. On my way out I decided to see what was new at the Redbox. In case they don't exist by the time this book gets into your hands, a Redbox is a giant vending machine for renting movies. You choose your movie, swipe your card, and like magic, out comes a DVD that you take home, watch, and return to a Redbox when you're done—unless you keep it too long, in which case you're now the proud owner of that movie. I have inadvertently purchased many subpar movies in my day because, as author Glennon Doyle says, "I can do hard things but not easy things," like return a Redbox DVD.[2]

At any rate, I was standing at the Redbox looking through the new releases and found a movie I wanted to see because I had heard it was amazing; I'd also heard that it had quite a bit of violence and graphic sexual content. I knew the kids would be in bed shortly after I got home, and I thought about how much I wanted to see said movie. I knew that the prophets had counseled us to not watch such films, but I don't really like being told what to do. I'm a rebel, remember? I began debating with myself about whether I should rent this movie. This was my model:

> **Circumstance:** Movie with gratuitous violence and sexual content.
> **Thought:** I know I've been advised not to watch things like this, but this one time won't affect me.
> **Feeling:** Justified.
> **Action:** I am inconsistent in aligning with the Spirit.
> **Result:** I get inconsistent results in my spiritual life.

I started finding plenty of justification for watching the movie and was about to get it, and then I was struck with an insight: What if I thought about the commandments in the same way I think about building a business? Why am I not applying the advice I just gave those new coaches to the most important goals of all—my eternal, spiritual health and progress? Avoiding inappropriate media is not advice from someone who is trying to control me or make my life less enjoyable. It's a strategy. All of the commandments—they are strategies.

These strategies help us reach our most important goals: to become like our Heavenly Parents, to make this life as enjoyable as possible along the way, to feel good when we can, to know how to cope when we feel bad, and to become higher versions of ourselves in the process. Our goal is not to avoid falling down but to get back up when we do fall, as we inevitably will. The challenge is that we are human beings in human bodies with human brains. We will be tempted in numerous ways. At times we will run into problems that we can't avoid, and we will create trials for ourselves and others despite our best intentions. But to help us overcome these challenges, we've been given strategies by someone who has already achieved what we're working toward, not unlike an online business mentor who has already created a highly successful business.

It's our Savior, Jesus Christ.

He has already done it and He is offering the way to us.

He came to earth and experienced what we're experiencing. Do we trust him? Do we follow His advice, or do we question it, saying, "That won't work for me. It's too hard. I don't want to"? In John 14:21–23, the Savior explains that following His teachings is about more than obedience; it's about giving love to Him and allowing ourselves to receive God's love: "He that hath my commandments, and keepeth them, he it is that loveth me; and he that loveth me shall be loved of my Father, and I will love him, and will manifest myself to him. . . . If a man love me, he will keep my words: and my Father will love him and we will come unto him, and make our abode with him."

The commandment to follow Him has more to do with the intent of our hearts. It is an offering of love to Him, a trust in Him, and a desire to follow Him. This righteous intent can transform us in powerful ways in this lifetime. I don't believe that following Christ means abiding by a prescriptive set of rules. I don't believe it means we are not expected to think for ourselves. The commandments are often nuanced and ambiguous because their application depends on individual choices and specific circumstances.

As I stood at the Redbox, I suddenly saw it all plainly before me: I do like being told what to do if I'm trying to accomplish a goal and I trust that the people advising me know what they're talking about. It's true that the suggestion to avoid certain types of movies is not doctrine, but the advice comes from a prophet of God and I can see how it aligns with the values I try to live by. I have plenty of self-discipline when I have bought into the reasons why, like I did with building my business. Who do I trust more than my Heavenly Parents and my Savior? Nobody. I may not think that watching a film like this will hold me back, and maybe it won't. But by trusting and following the advice of my business mentors I was able to create a multimillion-dollar business. Why wouldn't I want to approach my eternal goals with this same consistency and trust in the Lord? This is when I found a new model:

> **Circumstance:** Movie with gratuitous violence and sexual content.
> **Thought:** If the Lord says this won't serve me, I trust that.
> **Feeling:** Committed.
> **Action:** I follow the commandments more closely and create space in myself for the Spirit.
> **Result:** I am progressing spiritually the way I want to.

As I mentioned earlier, every week on Friday mornings I publish a podcast episode. In the beginning, when nobody was listening to my podcast except my mom and a few of my former coworkers, I still published every week. I published the week I had a baby. I publish even when it's late and I'm tired and I forgot to upload it, so I have to get out of bed and go downstairs to my computer and finish up. This is what my online business mentors told me to do, so I've done it, and it has paid off. To date, there have been more than fifteen million downloads of the podcast, which happened because I consistently showed up, offered my best, and asked people to rate and share it. Small things done consistently.

My guess is that I will achieve my spiritual and eternal goals in the same way. It won't be the big things I do or don't do that get me there. It will be the culmination of many little things that shape who I am, how I see the world, and the choices I make—"By small and simple things are great things brought to pass."[3] I walked out of the grocery store without renting that movie or any movie at all, because I remembered that I am a mother to young children and I can't stay awake past 9:30 p.m. to save my life. I would go home and read three pages of a book and nod off like I always do. But I will remember that the commandments are strategies. If I follow them, I am much more likely to get where I'm trying to go, and to get there more easily. In fact, I've already experienced this to be true.

I don't drink alcohol.

No, never.

Yes, really.

If you're a member of the Church who also doesn't drink alcohol, you won't find that hard to believe, and my guess is that you've had to explain the same thing to shocked people your entire life, just like I have. Because apparently alcohol is super fun. Or relaxing. I'm not sure, and I can't really relate to people's infatuation with it. Again, this is not because I am special in some way. It's only because I've never been a drinker, so my brain was never wired to crave alcohol.

If you don't expose yourself to concentrated hits of dopamine like the one people get when they drink alcohol, then you never internalize the model that keeps you coming back for more. The people who look at us with disbelief and confusion when we admit we never drink most likely have the following model:

Circumstance: Alcohol.

Thought: I want some of that.

Feeling: Desire.

Action: I drink alcohol, which gives me a dopamine hit and tells my brain that we should drink alcohol more often. Or, I resist the desire, which causes my brain to obsess about alcohol even more.

Result: My brain wants alcohol even more.

Now, to any of my alcohol-drinking friends who might be reading this book, please don't think I'm suggesting that any of us nondrinkers are more evolved or above you in some way. On the contrary, most of us have similar models about many other substances instead of alcohol. In the circumstance line of my models, rather than alcohol I have online shopping, Diet Coke, or old-fashioned glazed donuts. So if I want to rid myself of any of those habits, I have some work to do on my brain.

But alcohol is not something I have to work on, and again it's not because I am so wise and self-disciplined as to have never become hooked on it in the first place. It's only because I kept the commandment that told me not to drink it. I followed a single part of a single commandment (or strategy) that we call the Word of Wisdom, and it worked. That choice has made my life better. I know this because I have friends whom I love and adore who tell me that they wish they could stop drinking because they know it would make their lives better. Some of my friends have been successful, and others are still struggling to get there and talk about how challenging it is.

And believe me, friend, I do understand.

You're not weak.

You just have a human brain.

But I do look back at all those times in high school when I felt like the odd girl out because I *was* odd, but also because everyone except me was experimenting with alcohol. I think back to being the only girl at the party who was sober and wanting so desperately to be accepted by my peers. I think about all the corporate work retreats and dinners when everyone was enjoying themselves thanks to the wine and booze acting as liquid relaxation. Sometimes I was tempted to find out what all the fuss was about.

But I followed the Word of Wisdom strategy, and now that I've accepted my lack of coolness and have watched my peers wrestle with the desire to drink something that negatively impacts their health, their sleep, their focus, and their relationships, I am grateful that I have followed this commandment.

The Lord doesn't give us commandments to exert His authority. He isn't out to limit our fun or make our lives harder. He loves us and wants us to return to Him. He's trying to help us make our journey on earth as joy-filled as possible. And part of His effort includes guiding us away from choices that would cause the opposite of joy, as Elder ElRay L. Christiansen taught: "There are those who ask . . . , 'If the Lord loves us, why does he then give so many commandments, some of them restrictive in their nature?' Well, the answer is he gives us commandments because he loves us. He wishes to save us from sorrow and remorse and failure, and the worst of all, regret, and from losing our blessings."[4]

The Lord knows what will make it harder for us to achieve a joyful life and what will strengthen us spiritually, and that is why He's given us His counsel. Some people call His words commandments. I call them strategies. Game on.

---

1. Gretchen Rubin, *The Four Tendencies Quiz: Detailed Report: Rebel*, 2018, https://quiz.gretchenrubin.com/wp-content/uploads/2018/08/Rebel-Report.pdf.

2. Glennon Doyle, (@GlennonDoyle), "I can do hard things but not easy things and she KNOWS this," Twitter, June 13, 2019, 9:48 a.m., https://twitter.com/GlennonDoyle/status/1139197897986252800.

3. Alma 37:6.

4. ElRay L. Christiansen, "The Laws of God Are Blessings," *Ensign*, April 1975, https://www.churchofjesuschrist.org/study/general-conference/1975/04/the-laws-of-god-are-blessings?lang=eng.

Now I rejoice, not that ye were
made sorry, but that ye sorrowed to
repentance: for ye were sorry after a
godly manner, that ye might receive
damage by us in nothing.

2 Corinthians 7:9–10

08. REPENTANCE

I think I said this already, but I love TV.

I do.

I'm not ashamed to admit it, either.

Whenever I move into a new ward and get invited to the local ladies' book club, I have to refrain from asking, "Why can't we have a TV club?" I'd like to get together and discuss an episode of *Downton Abbey*, and I don't see how that's different from discussing a book. I know, I know, reading is better for your brain, but I grew up using TV to entertain, pass the time, be informed about the news, and keep me company. When I moved away to college and felt homesick, David Letterman was there on the TV, and watching him felt like home. Thanks, Dave. And when it comes to TV, rather than choose from the approximately 5,375 channels we have, I usually just put on a good home makeover show.

Yes, I know what this means.

I am old and also a nerd.

But regardless, who doesn't love the satisfying before and after of a makeover? I *have* to watch the end of *Fixer Upper* and see what amazing things Chip and Joanna have done.

"I hope they are going to like it," my husband and I joke, because we know that the family whose house is getting a Chip and Joanna upgrade will love it every time. But I still have to watch because the "before" has created an open loop in my brain that demands closure with an "after," and isn't it satisfying to see? It's satisfying because the before is usually a huge disaster, and the after . . . well . . . the after is nothing short of perfection.

Seriously.

Perfection.

My brain loves the perfection of those newly renovated, professionally designed, and Joanna Gaines–staged homes. They are perfect. But do you know why?

Nobody lives there yet.

The family hasn't been inside for more than a few minutes when we get the big reveal. Most of the things they own are not even in the house because they removed everything in order to renovate. Not a single child has come home from school, dropped his backpack on the floor, and kicked his shoes off on one side of the room and socks on the other as he excitedly tells Mom about what happened on the bus ride home. There are no dishes in the sink because no family has gathered around for a quick Crock-Pot dinner before a parent rushes one child off to dance and another off to a youth activity. There is no toothpaste in the sink from the child who is still learning how to spit properly. That untouched house is fun to look at, but we don't want it to stay that perfect. We want people to live there, and let's face it.

People are messy.

We're messy on the outside, and we're messy on the inside.

We're a complicated combination of past memories and future dreams. We are emotions and thoughts and bodies walking around trying to feel safe and happy and wondering why it's so hard to do. This human thing is no joke. When our Heavenly Parents sent us to earth, They knew our time here was going to be tough, and They knew that in our attempts to feel better about ourselves and this entire journey, we were going to fall down. Not only did They know it but that is part of the plan. They didn't know it in a "Let's plan for the worst and hope for the best" sort of way. They knew it in a "First I'll command them to obey, then they will disobey, and they will have the opportunity to repent because of the Atonement, and that is the plan" kind of way.

Elder Allen D. Haynie of the Seventy explained, "Before we came to this earth, we participated as spirit sons and daughters of God in a grand council. Each of us was paying attention and none of us fell asleep. In that council our Father in Heaven presented a plan. Because the plan preserved our agency and required that we learn from our own experience and not just from His, He knew we would commit sin."[1] In our premortal life, we knew that we'd make mistakes, and we accepted that. We can accept it in our earthly life, too. We can acknowledge our mistakes, be compassionate with ourselves, and keep trying.

Because falling down is part of the plan, the plan makes provision for the messes we will create for ourselves and for others. Falling down and then getting back up (in other words, repenting) strengthens us—just as a baby learning to walk gains the strength to do so by falling down and getting up repeatedly. Think about it. That baby is doing little baby squats all day until, eventually, walking gets easier.

Falling down and getting back up strengthens us emotionally, mentally, and spiritually. Our Heavenly Parents formulated a brilliant plan. Now, I don't know about you, but for me this thought sometimes creates a conundrum in my brain because part of the plan is that we are supposed to sin. Kind of. God gave us commandments to obey, and our Divine Parents genuinely want us to obey them. But They also know that sometimes we won't, and They genuinely love us just as much. And in Their wisdom and love, They gave us a gift to make this perfect plan work.

That gift is the Atonement of Jesus Christ, and it means that we can repent and have a do-over as many times as necessary.

Perfection seems like the goal. At church, we talk about the things we should be doing or the things we shouldn't be doing. We are constantly striving to do better and be better. We want our kids to obey, and we have a long list of ideas about how our spouses could improve. But perfection is impossible. It never was the plan. Constantly chasing down perfection is exhausting, and as we do so, we run right into the trap of shame.

Once you fall into the trap of shame, the shame keeps you stuck there. It is the belief that "something is wrong with me," and that is a lie. We all believe that lie from time to time, but it is not useful. According to shame researcher Brené Brown, shame leads to addiction, depression, violence, aggression, bullying, suicide, and eating disorders.[2] And most importantly, shame denies our divine heritage. We were all created by a loving Heavenly Father, and our value and worth is a given.

Every single one of us has value.

Equally.

We are all amazing and complete and worthy of love, and none of us had anything to do with it. So, there is nothing we can do and nothing that could happen to any of us that would diminish our value. It's simply not possible. But shame doesn't want you to understand that. Shame tells you the opposite. Spencer W. Kimball said it this way: "God is your Father. He loves you. He and your Mother in heaven value you beyond any measure. . . . You are unique. One of a kind, made of the eternal intelligence which gives you claim upon eternal life. Let there be no question in your mind about your value as an individual. The whole intent of the gospel plan is to provide an opportunity for each of you to reach your fullest potential, which is eternal progression and the possibility of godhood."[3]

When we sin, it's tempting to believe that we are now "less than." When I coach clients who feel this way, I suggest that they could choose to believe that they are no less now than they were before they sinned. They almost always tell me the same thing—that it doesn't seem right or fair to stop beating themselves up. I respond, of course, by saying that we can easily see if that thought is useful by putting it in a model.

Let's take a look at an example of a model we might see in a young person today:

> **Circumstance:** I had premarital sex.
> **Thought:** I am a terrible person.
> **Feeling:** Shame.
> **Action:** I don't tell anyone because I am afraid of what they will think or what will happen. I lie to my parents. I lie to my bishop so I can still go on a mission and not disappoint anyone. I ruminate about it and feel terrible. I am short with people around me. I am defensive and judgmental of others.
> **Result:** I am acting like a terrible version of myself.

This is a common model for a young person in this circumstance. The shameful thoughts lead to more problems because shame tells us we should hide. Obviously, shame is not useful, but the good news is that it's not our only option.

Remember the night I woke up from the dream in which I was about to die alone in a helicopter over the ocean? Not long after that night I found myself going through a repentance process of my own and wondering how I could possibly feel *godly* sorrow. We're told that to truly repent we must feel godly sorrow, and I imagined that it must be the deepest, most intense kind of sorrow there could possibly be. In my attempts to feel this way, I created so much shame over the mistakes I had made that I couldn't see a way out. I kept telling myself that I was a terrible, weak person, and even though I was working with my bishop and trying to go through the repentance process, I couldn't stop thinking about the choices I had made and the person I had become. My bishop told me that I would know when I was forgiven because I would feel a tremendous relief, like a weight off my shoulders. I did not feel that way, and I thought I never would.

One day on my way home from a work trip in Phoenix, I was running late to the airport and still had to return my rental car. At the Phoenix airport, the car rentals are in the underground parking lot, so I returned my car there and then headed toward the escalator that led to the top, where a shuttle bus would take me to the terminal. I was rolling my suitcase with one hand and my laptop roller bag with the other. As I neared the escalator, I briefly noticed a sign that read "If carrying luggage, please use the elevator," but being in a rush, I ignored it and stepped onto the escalator. Seconds after stepping on . . . I fell.

Not a cute little fall, like when you sort of catch yourself and hope nobody notices.

A legitimate, on my back, feet above my head, unable to get up sort of fall. I struggled to get up for about twenty to thirty seconds, which felt like an eternity as people watched in horror, unable to assist me. Every time I started to get up, I would fall again. Over and over and over. It was mortifying. Fortunately, I was not hurt once I finally made it to my feet, but I was in a bit of shock and a great deal of humiliation. People asked me if I was OK and then tried to leave me alone to shake off the embarrassment, but I could not believe what had just happened. I made it to the top of the moving stairs, hopped on the shuttle bus, and began replaying the incident in my mind.

And then I saw it.

I understood why I had gone down in the first place and why I couldn't get up.

I was rolling two bags behind me, and they didn't fit together into the narrow escalator entrance, so they pulled me down once I stepped on. Every time I tried to get up, those bags pulled me down again because I was clinging tightly to them the entire time. It wasn't until they finally shimmied their way into that narrow stairway that I was finally able to get up. If I had only let go of those bags right after falling, I would have been able to get right up with no problem.

Why had I held on to them?

The trauma of the moment had created a lack of access to my rational brain, so it seemed important to hold on to the luggage. Without my conscious brain seeing the bigger picture, my unconscious brain knew that my valuable things were in those bags and that I should hold on tight to them and not lose them. I didn't have the time or calm thinking abilities to consider that I could easily go back down and get those bags or that someone would likely bring them up to me. In reality, being safe on the escalator was more of a priority. I should have just let go of those bags.

Moments after I had that realization on that shuttle bus heading to the Phoenix airport, I felt the Spirit tap me on the shoulder again. Just as I'd felt it that night in my bedroom. I thought about the repentance process I was going through, and this thought entered my mind: *Let go of the baggage.* The baggage I was holding on to was shame. It was like two huge roller bags, and every time I tried to stand up, shame pulled me back down again. Shame told me that God was disappointed in me, which resulted in me feeling very disconnected from Him. Shame told me that good people don't do what I'd done, and therefore, I was not a good person. Shame told me not to pray . . . at least not with sincerity. Shame was heavy, and it felt important and necessary, but I could not stand up and move forward as long as I was holding on to it.

I began crying right then and there on the shuttle bus as I realized what godly sorrow really is. Godly sorrow is not an intense, shame-filled, self-loathing depression. It is the opposite of that. It is not, "I'm sorry I'm so terrible." It is, "I'm sorry . . . that's not who I am." Godly sorrow is a recognition that the way you acted is not who you really are because all "bad" behavior is based in fear, and you are not fear. You are made in God's image, and God is love. Therefore you, my friend, are love as well.

Elder Dieter F. Uchtdorf gave a beautiful definition of godly sorrow that resonates with me, especially considering my experience of being pulled down before finally getting on my feet again:

> The Apostle Paul taught that "godly sorrow worketh repentance to salvation . . . but the sorrow of the world worketh death."[4] Godly sorrow inspires change and hope through the Atonement of Jesus Christ. Worldly sorrow pulls us down, extinguishes hope, and persuades us to give in to further temptation.
>
> Godly sorrow leads to conversion and a change of heart. It causes us to hate sin and love goodness. It encourages

us to stand up and walk in the light of Christ's love. True repentance is about transformation, not torture or torment.[5]

Even if one day you find yourself in a serious repentance process, please know that your worth is never in question. You don't have to do anything to earn or prove your value. It just is. Doctrine and Covenants 18:10 tells us to "Remember the worth of souls is great in the sight of God." We can confuse ourselves about this truth because sometimes our choices leave us unworthy to participate in certain ordinances, but that doesn't change our worth. As Joy D. Jones explains, *worthiness* and *worth* have different meanings: "Let me point out the need to differentiate between two critical words: worth and worthiness. They are not the same. Spiritual *worth* means to value ourselves the way Heavenly Father values us, not as the world values us. Our worth was determined before we ever came to this earth.

"On the other hand, *worthiness* is achieved through obedience. If we sin, we are less worthy, but we are never worth less! We continue to repent and strive to be like Jesus with our worth intact."[6]

Shame says that our houses, and our lives, should remain in perfect, staged condition at all times and that if they don't, something is wrong. But the truth is we were never meant for perfection. We are meant for messes. Messes we create in our homes and in our lives and within ourselves. It's not intentional. We still want to strive to be more loving, more honest, and more like our Savior, but in this life we will never achieve perfection. That doesn't mean something is wrong. It means that God's plan is working just as it was designed.

I don't think of repentance in the same way I used to. I used to think repentance was something we did to be punished or to suffer in order to compensate for our mistakes. But of course that is not necessary or even possible. The only one who is able to compensate already did so. He is our Savior, Jesus Christ. When we repent, it's to realign ourselves with Him and with who we truly are, which is a loving son or daughter of a loving God.

You know when you're using a mouse with your computer, and you end up at the edge of the mousepad? You have to pick up the mouse and move it back to the middle to navigate the screen again. But you don't get mad at the mouse or at yourself for ending up on the edge. You just pick up the mouse and put it back where it belongs. This is the way with repentance. It's a realignment with who we truly are, and our ability to do so is a generous gift. Thinking of repentance this way doesn't mean we justify bad behavior. Sin is sin. But shame is not a part of the repentance process. Godly sorrow is "I am a son/daughter of God. I can do better."

Let's go back to our made-up example and find a more useful model:

Circumstance: I had premarital sex.

Thought: I am just as valuable and complete as I was before, and I can do better.

Feeling: Godly sorrow.

Action: I repent. I stop repeating my mistake in my head. I begin focusing on a better future. I have space within myself to serve others because I am a complete person.

Result: I am more patient and less judgmental of myself and others.

Shame is Satan's way of keeping you in the trap of sin. Shame encourages more sin. It keeps you stuck on the edge of that mousepad. But perfect people and perfect houses are not a thing in the real world. They are temporary. They are supposed to mess up and get messed up again and again. The baggage we hold on to after we have fallen feels important. A part of your brain believes it is somehow righteous to keep getting pulled down by it, and Satan plays on that belief when he can. But this is a lie. You are allowed to let go, stand up, and move on. This is what the Lord wants for you and for me. Don't fall into the addictive and toxic trap of shame. Remember, you are a loving, creative, service-oriented being at your core. Find your way back to this part of you with the Lord's help. This is repentance.

---

1. Allen D. Haynie, "Remembering in Whom We Have Trusted," *Ensign*, October 2015, https://www.churchofjesuschrist.org/study/general-conference/2015/10/remembering-in-whom-we-have-trusted?lang=eng.

2. Brené Brown, "Listening to Shame," March 2012, TED video, 20:23 (quote at 14:20), https://www.ted.com/talks/brene_brown_listening_to_shame?language=en.

3. Spencer W. Kimball, "Privileges and Responsibilities of Sisters," Ensign, November 1978, 105, https://www.churchofjesuschrist.org/study/general-conference/1978/10/privileges-and-responsibilities-of-sisters?lang=eng.

4. 2 Corinthians 7:10.

5. Dieter F. Uchtdorf, "You Can Do It Now!" Ensign, October 2013, https://www.churchofjesuschrist.org/study/general-conference/2013/10/you-can-do-it-now?lang=eng.

6. Joy D. Jones, "Value Beyond Measure," Ensign, October 2017, https://www.churchofjesuschrist.org/study/general-conference/2017/10/value-beyond-measure?lang=eng.

A new commandment I give unto you,
That ye love one another; as I have
loved you, that ye also love
one another.

John 13:34

09. LOVE ONE ANOTHER

L et's talk about love.

Love can be a surprisingly complicated topic, partly because our language about love is so imprecise. We use the word *love* to describe too many things. It can mean romantic attraction: "I think I'm in love." It can mean strong preference: "I love that color on you." It can mean loyal commitment: "Their life is a beautiful love story." It can mean admiration: "I really love what she's made of her life." We use the word *love* as both noun and verb. Its meaning spans from fleeting and trite to lasting and profound. The Greeks knew that one word wasn't enough for the profound experiences we have with love. They had a word for romantic/sexual love (*eros*), another for affection between friends (*philia*), another for familial love (*storge*), and another for unconditional love or charity (*agape*).

So although the word itself falls short at times, few would disagree that love can be a healing and transformative force in the world. Christ taught and demonstrated this kind of love. For the purposes of this chapter, think of love as an emotion most of us want to live from more frequently. Love goes in our model's feeling line, which means that it is created by loving thoughts.

And love not only feels great but also fuels loving actions that create loving results. When we feel the emotion of love, it is a win for us and everyone around us. "Love others as I have loved you" is a beautiful commandment. But, in practice, loving one another can be a challenge. Of all the issues I coach my clients on, their ability to love everyone is by far the most frequent topic, and my clients are amazing, kind people who truly desire to love others. So if we're commanded to love one another, and we desire it, then why is it so tough to do sometimes?

Yes to People

My first job ever was as a hostess at the Old Spaghetti Factory. I was so excited to get that job. I applied the day I turned sixteen because I couldn't wait to work to earn my own money, contribute to the world in some way, and be a part of a team with goals. In my role as a hostess, I was expected to follow certain policies and procedures, which were written down in the employee manual. I had to wear a dress or skirt to work. I was expected to greet customers in a certain way and answer the phone a particular way. My managers expected me to show a certain level of professionalism and kindness toward my coworkers and our customers. Failure to follow these policies could result in disciplinary action, "up to and including termination," as the attorneys and HR executives like to say.

This manual for being a hostess at the Old Spaghetti Factory was useful. It helped me understand what my boss expected of me, and it helped me know how to succeed. I was being paid to show up a certain way, and I was willing to follow the rules. In an employment situation, it's simple: follow the expectations and then you get to keep your job and get paid; don't follow them and you ultimately lose your job. But in our personal relationships, we use "manuals" to create problems for ourselves. In our minds, we create manuals of expectations for the people in our lives, and then we tie our emotions to their adherence to the manual. *Be the way I believe you should be, and then I'll be happy. If you act differently, I will be unhappy and blame you for it.*

I was born of goodly parents. I say this not to compare myself to Nephi but rather to compare my parents, Jeff and Bonnie Lyman, to Lehi and Sariah. I have amazing parents.

As my siblings and I were growing up, our father taught us the importance of serving and loving others. He taught us through his words but more profoundly through his actions. When I was a teenager, my dad was into biking; after his long rides he could often be found in the garage cleaning and tuning every part of his extremely loved, and expensive, bike. One Saturday my friends and I wanted to go mountain biking, but one of those friends didn't have a bike. When I suggested that she could probably ride my dad's bike, she was hesitant. When he told her she was welcome to use it she said, "But Brother Lyman, that bike is your pride and joy," to which he replied, "No, you kids are my pride and joy. That is just a bike."

My mother was no less impressive in her own way. As teenagers, my sister and I had a moment when we realized we would never measure up to her. My sister pointed this out one summer day when we were sitting in our home having a casual lunch together. We were eating delicious sandwiches that my mom had made for us. She had baked the homemade bread, and we were using plates that she had hand-painted at a local ceramics store. She can sew, bake, wrap a gift like you've never seen, and she was always busy serving in a Church calling or volunteering in the community, all while raising her five children.

Of course, my parents are not perfect, but I have always looked to them as great examples. They were wonderful role models to me, and by watching them I created a picture of what a husband-and-wife relationship should look like. My dad was always the rational, logical one. He was steady and calm in the face of a crisis, saying things like, "Let's gather the facts," and "It's only money." He worked hard and loved doing it. His career was a big part of his identity. Mom was the nurturing and more emotional one who cried when she was very happy or very frustrated or feeling the Spirit, which balanced our home and brought a sort of humanness in contrast to my dad's seemingly stoic demeanor. This picture of my parents is lovely isn't it? It is. Except when I used it to create problems for myself in my own marriage.

My husband, Jake, is amazing. Really. I'm not just saying that. He is the kind of guy who says on the way to church, "Thanks for doing such a great job getting ready and out the door today, kids." He considers putting together a piece of IKEA furniture to be fun—he calls it high-stakes Legos. Today I love him with all of my heart. But there were times in our marriage when I wasn't as good at loving him. In the beginning I thought he was doing it all wrong.

Jake is sensitive. He's patient and kind and has a tender heart. He feels emotions intensely, so it's not uncommon for him to get choked up or even cry when he is very happy or very frustrated or feeling the Spirit. This was confusing to me at first because I thought that was my role as the wife and that he was supposed to be more like my dad. He was supposed to be the rational, strong voice of reason. In the beginning of our marriage, I was uncomfortable with this. It seemed that he was playing the role of the husband incorrectly.

He worried and stressed about things much more than I did.

He was uncertain of himself at times.

He struggled for a while to find his way in his career and then went through emotional highs and lows as he worked to support us. It's not that he couldn't do it. He can and has done it amazingly well, but he didn't love it like my dad seemed to love his career. Jake was not following the guidelines in my unwritten, unspoken, even unconscious husband manual. If he had been my employee I would have sat down with him to go through the manual and explain how he was falling short, preventing my happiness. But he wasn't my employee. So I just resented him instead.

Of course in reality, he was never doing it wrong. He was just being himself. I was the only one who needed to change. I wanted him to be someone different than he was so that he'd comply with the manual I had created in my head. Meanwhile, I was wrestling with my own demons over my love of working outside the home. My children always preferred their dad over me when they were injured or emotional because he was the one who knew best how to be gentle and kind in these situations. I couldn't make myself do so many of the things that I'd appreciated about my own mom as I was growing up, like making family dinners, decorating for every holiday, or canning peaches. Turns out I had created a manual not only for husbands, which Jake didn't comply with, but also for wives, which was a far cry from who I was as well.

Do you know what happens when you combine shame with blame? I'll tell you. You spin in unhappiness and powerlessness. One minute you're judging the person you believe is responsible for your pain, and the next minute you're judging yourself. Your brain becomes confused about whose fault "this" is, and you have little hope of getting out of the spin because it turns out that "this" is nobody's fault. Because "this" isn't even a real problem. It's just the Something Has Gone Wrong brain software running again. The way out is actually quite simple. The way out is to let go of your expectations of that person you want to love.

I still remember the conversation that set me on a different path. I was talking with a friend who is good at telling me the truth, and I told her how I just wanted to see Jake reach his potential because I could see that he had so much. She looked at me and said, "When are you going to stop cheating on your husband with your husband's potential?" She didn't mean literally; she meant in my head. I was in love with a slightly different version of Jake, which I had made up, and as a result I was making myself miserable and disconnecting in my marriage. So that day I decided to be wrong—wrong about what husbands and wives and marriages and families are supposed to look like. I decided to allow Jake to be Jake and me to be me. As I made this shift, which took some time by the way, I realized that Heavenly Father had given us everything we needed in our family. I am like my dad, and Jake has a lot of the qualities I love about my mom. And even if he didn't, he is a human and completely worthy of love no matter what. He is 100 percent loveable just as he is. I just had to get better at the skill of loving to see it.

Think about the person in your life who is the most challenging to love. Do you have someone in mind? Maybe it's your sister-in-law, a former business partner, or someone you know through your kids' school; it might even be your spouse or child. Now, ask yourself what expectation of yours this person is not living up to. Perhaps you want them to be more interested in your life, to be less critical, to stop talking about themselves so

150

much, to parent the kids more like you do, or to do what they say they are going to do.

These sound like reasonable expectations to have, but if they prevent you from loving this person, then the expectations are not useful because they are keeping you from feeling curious, connected, or loving. It is not our job to create manuals for how other people should behave in order for us to love them. It's not what Christ teaches. It is not what He demonstrated for us when He was on earth, and part of the reason He came was to give us an example to follow. Christ loves people regardless of whether they have behaved themselves. President Thomas S. Monson reminded us of this when he said, "God's love is there for you whether or not you feel you deserve love. It is simply always there."[1]

The Lord does not have manuals for any of us, because He is perfect at the skill of loving. He demonstrated this when a woman caught in the act of adultery was brought to Him and He replied, "He that is without sin among you, let him first cast a stone at her."[2] But even when others' behavior isn't as blatantly wrong as the sin for which this woman was accused, we struggle to love them because we believe we know how others should behave.

Jane, one of my clients, told me that her mother didn't spend much time with her grandchildren. Jane's mother would visit on occasion but overall didn't seem up for watching the kids or coming to their games or performances. Jane couldn't believe that a grandmother wouldn't want to be more involved in her grandkids' lives. She had a manual for how good grand-mothers should behave, which included attending her grandkids' extracurricular activities, wanting to do projects with them, and spending time with them in various ways. Because her mother didn't follow this manual, Jane felt resentful toward her instead of loving her. She felt sure that if her mom would just be differ-ent, then it would be easier to love her. Here is Jane's model:

Circumstance: Mom didn't come to the kids' soccer game on Saturday.

Thought: She is not being a good grandma.

Feeling: Resentful.

Action: Ruminate about what she's doing wrong. Gossip about her to my siblings. Stew about it instead of enjoying the soccer game. Act distracted and grumpy when my kids try to talk to me.

Result: I am not being the kind of mom/daughter I want to be.

I pointed out to Jane that her mother seemed to have a full life and a variety of things she wanted to spend her time doing. If Jane wanted to, she could love her mom just as she is. We want people to be different so we can love them, but if they change for us, then we are not loving them. We are loving a pretend version of them. We disconnect from people and the experience of knowing them when we are fixated on how they are "doing it wrong." Our behavior starts to reflect the very things we are judging them for; in other words, I am not acting like a great mom when I think my mom is not a good grandmother. I am judging my sister when I think, "She shouldn't judge." We are the ones who are being negative when we tell our friends about our negative husbands. The alternative is to accept that people get to be whoever they want to be, and we can choose to love them—exactly as they are. Here's a new model for Jane to try:

Circumstance: Mom didn't come to the kids' soccer game on Saturday.

Thought: I love her, and I am glad she has a full life.

Feeling: Love.

Action: I am happy and present during the game and when I'm with my mom.

Result: I love my life.

When I teach this concept to my clients they often say, "OK, Jody, so you're telling me I shouldn't have *any* expectations of people?" I tell them they can have expectations if they want to, and I've found that any expectation I have that aligns with who the person already is or is striving to be can be useful in a relationship. For example, I expect that my husband never hits me, and he doesn't ever hit me, so that's a match. And if he did start hitting me, that would be a deal breaker and I would need to figure out how to leave this relationship. He expects me not to swear at him, and I choose not to swear at him, so again we have a match. But if the people in our lives aren't living up to our expectations, then we have choices to make. They are not easy choices, and I'm not trying to diminish the complicated nature of relationships, but we can choose whether we will stay or go, whether we will allow a behavior or walk away, whether we will lovingly hold people accountable (when appropriate) or silently resent them. All of these decisions are ours to make, and every one of them can be made from a place of love. Resentment and anger are not our only options. Love is a choice you can make, and it's always the best one.

A client once asked me, "You say we can love people even when they misbehave, but what does that even look like?" and I told her, "Well, it looks exactly like Jesus Christ." This is how Christ lived when He was on the earth. He demonstrated it for us then and continues to love us now. Love can be challenging, and many of us will spend our lives learning how to love others as Christ loves them. But it is so worth it, as President Gordon B. Hinkley so beautifully explained:

> Love is the very essence of life. It is the pot of gold at the end of the rainbow. Yet it is more than the end of the rainbow. Love is at the beginning also, and from it springs the

beauty that arches across the sky on a stormy day. Love is the security for which children weep, the yearning of youth, the adhesive that binds marriage, and the lubricant that prevents devastating friction in the home; it is the peace of old age, the sunlight of hope shining through death. How rich are those who enjoy it in their associations with family, friends, church and neighbors.[3]

Remember, though, that loving people doesn't mean condoning bad behavior. It doesn't mean we don't teach the people whom we have a responsibility for teaching (such as our kids). It doesn't even mean that we don't make requests of other people, set boundaries, or leave a relationship. It only means that hatred, frustration, and anger don't have to be the fuel for our actions. Love feels better and is more effective.

Recently I had the opportunity to go on an amazing trip to Punta Mita, Mexico, just outside Puerto Vallarta. It was a once-in-a-lifetime sort of vacation. I was invited on the trip by friends who had rented the most beautiful villa on the beach, and it came with our own personal guide named Alejandro. From the moment we woke up until we retired to bed, Alejandro was there to get us anything we wanted anytime we wanted it. Bringing us food and beverages, placing beach chairs in a particular location, finding a random board game we wanted to play, getting the iguana out of our pool . . . you name it, to any request we made of him Alejandro said, "*Claro que si*." It was surreal to be waited on in this manner; none of us were accustomed to this type of treatment. We were curious about people who live this way regularly, and we had quite a few questions for Alejandro.

"What's the most bizarre request anyone has made of you?" we asked.

"An elephant on the beach," he told us.

"What? Were you able to get one?"

"*Claro que si.*"

"Does your wife miss you because you work such long days?"

"She is happy for the money, and I get several days off in a row between shifts."

"Are people ever mean to you?"

"No," he said without hesitation.

"Really? Never? You must get some people who come through here who are entitled and not terribly nice to you. Nobody is rude? Really?"

Alejandro shook his head and simply said, "I understand why people behave the way they do sometimes. Sometimes people are struggling. I just love people."

And there it is, my friends. Wisdom from Alejandro of Punta Mita. The way he thinks about people is pure gold. It creates the way he feels and the way he interacts with other people. He didn't describe his thoughts in this way—he may not even realize that he created them. He may believe that only kind people stay in his villa, but I assure you this is not the case because we were able to gather several stories from Alejandro that would suggest otherwise. His love of people comes from the way he chooses to think about people. He doesn't expect them to behave in any certain way. He has compassion for the ones who are struggling and who behave "badly" as a result. This compassion is what Christ demonstrates. In John 12:47 He says, "And if any man hear my words, and believe not, I judge him not: for I came not to judge the world, but to save the world." This is loving one another.

Do It for You

I coach many individuals who are trying to love someone who they believe is a difficult person. They often tell me that they know they "should" love this person but that they just can't or don't really know how. It feels important and justified to be resentful or even angry. They say they know they are supposed to choose love but that, truthfully, sometimes they don't really want to because they believe this person doesn't deserve their love. To them it feels like it would be unfair to love the misbehaving person because it would somehow reward the behavior.

The first thing I tell these clients is that they must allow themselves to feel whatever emotions they are feeling. Take a deep breath, relax into the feelings, and don't be mad at yourself for being mad at someone else. But then once the emotion settles down (which always happens more quickly by allowing it than by resisting it), I tell my clients in these situations that they have it all backward. They are confused about the commandment we've been given to love one another. We were never told "You should love other people for their sake"; we are simply told to love one another, and I believe this commandment (like every other one) is as much for our benefit as it is for the benefit of others. We think, "Oh yeah, I should love people for their sake, and as a small bonus I'll feel better too." But maybe it's more accurate to think, "Oh yeah, I am going to love people for my sake, and as a bonus I'll be putting more love into the world, and that is a very good thing."

Let's talk about love as an emotion that you feel in your body. Love feels amazing—warm, full, and peaceful. It feels like completeness and it feels like reverence. It's a warmth that dances around your heart, soothes your stomach, increases your lung capacity, and sharpens your focus on all that is light and good. Love is something that *you* feel in *your* body when you're feeling it. It must be what God feels, and what Christ felt in abundance when He was on earth and still feels today.

When you are living from a model that contains love, it will be a win for everyone, but when you *feel* love, you benefit. That wonderful feeling doesn't jump out of your body and into the body of the person you are loving. We could have a debate about whether we can feel one another's feelings, and we could discuss the energetic field that transmits love; I would agree that there is a lot of truth to that idea. But for now I want to focus on the idea that when you choose love you get to feel one of the most expansive feelings available to us in this life. In fact, the object of your love is quite irrelevant. You could be feeling love for your house or for your car. You could feel it for the weather. You could feel it for yourself. Or you could feel it for other people. When you feel love, you win because love is you—free from the bonds of mortality. Free from temptation. Free from fear. Free from shame. Free from all of the emotions that limit you and prevent you from achieving your potential in this life. And this is only the beginning of the good news.

When you're feeling love you will show up as a loving person. This is where it gets complicated, though. Love can say yes, but sometimes love says no. Love can stay, but sometimes love says leave. And while I previously described love as a great feeling, we all know that sometimes love leads us to pain or sadness or causes us to suffer alongside others. Again, love is extremely complex. Regardless, operating from the emotion of love is always in our best interest. And, as Elder Joseph B. Wirthlin taught, choosing love is also necessary for our spiritual growth: "The gospel of Jesus Christ is a gospel of transformation. It takes us as men and women of the earth and refines us into men and women for the eternities. The means of this refinement is our Christlike love. There is no pain it cannot soften, no bitterness it cannot remove, no hatred it cannot alter. The Greek playwright Sophocles wrote: 'One word frees us of all the weight and pain of life: That word is love.'"[4]

Does that "difficult" person deserve your love? Well, he or she can't feel your love. You think loving thoughts and then your body releases neurochemicals like dopamine, oxytocin, and serotonin.[5] Other people can feel only their own emotions. Because just as our thoughts create our emotions, their thoughts create their emotions. When you begin showing up from a feeling of love many other people will experience you differently because your actions and demeanor will change. When people interact with you they may feel something positive but it will only be because of the thoughts they are thinking. Sometimes we punish ourselves by denying ourselves the feeling of love when someone behaves in a way we don't like. We all do it at times. But when we do this, we essentially punish ourselves for someone else's "bad" behavior.

Sometimes one of my children will be upset with me for a mean-mom thing I've done, like making them go to school or telling them to eat breakfast before they have ice cream. They'll tell me they don't like me, either with a look or with their words, and I'll reply, "But I love you, and there's nothing you can do about it." That's how I feel about love. It's my right, and I get to love anyone I want to. And loving people who are not loving me (at least in that moment) is one of my favorite things to do. We are more confident and empowered when we stay in a loving space. We are more effective at anything we are trying to accomplish. We have more courage, more wisdom, more solutions, and more patience. Love breeds goodness in us, and then we pass that goodness along through our actions. Love is truly us at our best.

Christ had a human experience, too. He came to earth, and multitudes of people loved Him, but many people did not. Some hated Him and were threatened by Him, but He didn't stop loving them just because they were wrong about Him. He understood that they were just confused. Sometimes people are confused. However, it is not easy to love people who have negative feelings toward us. It's work I expect I will have to keep practicing for the rest of my life.

My twelve-year-old daughter, Macy, is beginning to experience the challenges of girlfriend relationships that seem to become prevalent around this time in life. One day she came to me and in a somber tone shared that a couple of her friends had said something not nice about her to another friend. I flashed back to my own experiences with girlfriends and remembered the backbiting and gossiping that felt so important and distressing. I tried to hold a space for Macy to hurt and told her that I was so sorry she was in pain. I told her it is OK to be sad or worried about it, and I felt some sadness alongside her for a while.

Then I asked her if I could teach her something. I asked her because I know what it's like to want to hurt without someone giving you the solution to fix it. Sometimes being in the pain and with the pain *is* the way through the pain, and I didn't want to rob her of the experience if that was true for her. But she wanted to hear what I had to say, so I told her about love.

I told her that her friends' judgment was not creating her pain. Her own thoughts were creating her pain. I explained that the thoughts she's believed about her friends and about herself were being challenged but that this is actually good news. Because while we may not be able to control our friends' thoughts, we can always control our own thoughts about ourselves and about our friends.

She was interested in this idea, which surprised me because she is often not at all interested in what I want to teach her. So I took her interest as a cue to keep going.

"What do you think about you?" I asked her.

She looked confused and said, "Um, I don't know. What do you mean?"

"Do you like you?" I asked her.

She hesitantly nodded and I said, "Why? Tell me some things you like about you."

She replied that she feels she is a good person. She is honest and kind.

I added a few things of my own for her to consider: "Yes, I agree. Also you're super funny. You consider other people's feelings when you make decisions. You work hard at school. You bring a fun energy to our family."

She nodded her head, and I watched her demeanor begin to shift.

"And what do you think about those two girls who might have said something unkind about you? We don't know for sure if what they said is true, but it could be. What if it is? What do you think about them? Do you still love them?"

She looked sad again as she thought about this question. I asked her why people do and say mean things, and I asked if she thought whether people were feeling really good about themselves when they said things like this. She recognized that, no, that's probably not the case. We talked about how as human beings we sometimes do and say unkind things because a part of our brain thinks that these actions will somehow make us feel better.

We listed all the things we appreciate about these two girls, and we talked about how to set boundaries when needed. We explored the option of having a conversation with the girls about this situation if Macy wanted to. But I also explained that Macy is allowed to keep loving the girls if she wants to. She can have compassion for them and compassion for herself at the same time. I also reminded her that, if she wanted to, she could ask Heavenly Father to help her think compassionate thoughts instead of painful ones. She nodded, said thanks, and went to bed.

The next morning, Macy said something to me that she had never said before and has not said again about anything I've tried to teach her. Usually she says, "Don't try to life coach me," and I have to explain that I'm not being a life coach. I'm being her mom. But this time she said, "Mom, what we talked about last night was so helpful. I feel so much better today. I like me and I like them, and they just might be struggling right now. It feels much better. Thanks for teaching me that."

These thoughts don't just work for preteen drama, my friends. I teach the same concept in the same way and see the same transformation in adults who have stepmothers who judge them, friends at church who exclude them, family members who are mad at them, and sisters-in-law who ignore them. The scriptures remind us to "bless them that curse you, do good to them that hate you, and pray for them who despitefully use you and persecute you."[6] This teaching is not something that you "should" do because you are a better person if you do it. It's a strategy for feeling better, being more empowered in your own life, and creating the kind of relationships you want. It's for you.

When people are wrong about us, when people don't behave the way we are sure they should behave, and even when people let us down over and over again, we have two options:

1. We can be mad about it and punish ourselves in the hopes this will change these people (spoiler alert . . . it won't).

2. We can love them and do the hard work of loving ourselves (which is required to love people who are judging us), and in the process we evolve personally and get to feel love.

As far as I see it, those are our only options.

Which one will you choose?

By the way, I wrote a new manual for my husband, Jake. This is what it says:

Be Jake.

He follows it perfectly.

———————

1. Thomas S. Monson, "We Never Walk Alone," *Ensign*, November 2013, 124, https://abn.churchofjesuschrist.org/study/general-conference/2013/10/we-never-walk-alone?lang=eng.

2. John 8:1–11.

3. Gordon B. Hinckley, "And the Greatest of These Is Love," *Ensign*, March 1984, https://www.churchofjesuschrist.org/study/ensign/1984/03/and-the-greatest-of-these-is-love?lang=eng.

4. *Oedipus at Colonus*, in *The Oedipus Cycle*, trans. Dudley Fitts and Robert Fitzgerald (New York: Harcourt Brace & Company, 1949), 161–62.

5. Loretta G. Breuning, "The Neurochemistry of Love," *Psychology Today*, February 13, 2018, https://www.psychologytoday.com/us/blog/your-neurochemical-self/201802/the-neurochemistry-love.

6. 3 Nephi 12:44.

Remember the worth of souls is great
in the sight of God.

Doctrine and Covenants 18:10

10. INDIVIDUAL WORTH

Yes to All of You

Amazing.

That's what you are. No, really. You're a miracle that I can't even begin to wrap my mind around. The way you formed in your mother's belly, growing from a tiny dot to the sizes of various fruits, and then one day . . . there you were. A human. And in only nine-ish months? I don't know about you, but I have never created anything as miraculous as a human in nine months. It took me nine months to return something to Nordstrom once. An entire human being? Unbelievable.

Our bodies are amazing. Did you know your body builds a new intestinal tract every three to four days as cells die and are regenerated? Every three months your red blood cells die, and the kidney cells you have today are not the ones you had a year ago. According to scientists, your entire body is nearly completely regenerated every ten years.[1] There are a billion other amazing things our bodies do that I won't go into, but I hope you are considering for just a moment how amazing and brilliant and miraculous your body is.

Maybe your body looks like you think it should look, or maybe you believe it's too big in places or too small in places. Perhaps your body feels good to be in and you can do many things you want to do, or perhaps it's painful being in your body right now and you are limited. Bodies are complicated, and our thoughts about them are even more so. But nothing changes the truth, which is that your body is a miracle that is worth celebrating and being in awe of.

And then there is your spirit.

Wow.

Your spirit is amazing on a level that we don't have the slightest clue about. We don't really know how spirits work. We don't have scientific studies or evidence to take a look at, or even the ability to see or examine a spirit. We believe we are created by Heavenly Parents in their image,[2] and we know our spirits will keep living after our bodies die, but we don't know much beyond that. So perhaps one day we'll better understand the miracle of your spirit, but for today, let's settle on knowing that its value is incomprehensible.

Put a spirit and a body together and send it through the veil to forget the premortal existence, and we have you right about now. You in mortality. You as a human being living on planet Earth. You are nothing short of miraculous. This is true for you, and it's true for me. It's true for every person who has ever lived, and for everyone who will come to earth in the future. We are all amazing creations, and we are all of tremendous value.

And every one of us is incapable of fully comprehending this fact.

We wonder if perhaps other people are a little better than we are in some ways or if maybe we're just a little better than they are in other ways. We sometimes want this human experience to be a game or a race with winners and losers, and we want to compare ourselves to others to judge how we're doing. We have these uncertainties because we don't remember the truth. The truth is that every one of us is 100 percent loveable, complete, and miraculous and that we are all here on earth to fall down, to experience challenges and joy, and to grow.

That's it.

That's the truth.

We're supposed to be good at some things and bad at other things. We're supposed to make good choices and stupid choices. We're supposed to have strengths that our friends didn't get and weaknesses that our friends don't struggle with. We share some commonalities with one another, but we are all a unique combination of traits (both physical and intangible) that doesn't exist in any other person, ever. You may be reading this, nodding your head and thinking, "Yes, I know all of this. Tell me something I don't know." But here's the thing: You know this, but do you *know* this? Do you really accept all of this as truth, and do you examine yourself under this lens?

Or do you wish you were just a little better or different in some way?

Do you think it will be easier to like yourself once you're more thin, more patient with your kids, less selfish, more smart? Do you think that self-compassion lies on the other side of cleaning the house? Achieving a goal? Checking more off your to-do list? Maybe if you were more righteous, more regular with temple attendance, or more consistent with ministering? Would you feel better about yourself then?

If so, then congratulations, you are a human and a mentally healthy one at that. It's normal to think like this. But I want to point out that you are mistaken about the source of

167

your worth. You are amazing and "worthy" and valuable and complete, and you had nothing to do with it. You are divinely created in the image of Heavenly Parents, so you are inherently valuable. Nothing you do will change that. You can't increase or decrease your value. You can change only the experience you create for yourself in this life. If you want to, you can work to understand your worth more completely and temper the part of yourself that believes otherwise. And I highly recommend you do. To start, let's look at a model you might have right now.

> **Circumstance:** I didn't reach out to help someone I knew was struggling.
> **Thought:** If I were a better person I would have helped.
> **Feeling:** Shame.
> **Action:** I avoid the struggling friend because I am ashamed. I avoid thinking about her because I feel badly whenever I do. I am not great at seeing opportunities to help others because my focus is instead on myself and how I'm bad. I don't have as much to give because I'm struggling myself.
> **Result:** I prove to myself that I'm not as good of a person as I should be.

When we are filled with self-loathing or shame, we do not do better. We might get a temporary surge of motivation to improve, but our action will be forced, disingenuous, and short-lived. Shame is a focus on self and a focus on what's wrong with ourselves at that. It requires that we protect ourselves. It requires reinforcement of our story about ourselves. When we think we are not good, we perpetuate our story about how we are not good, because, as it always does, what is in our thought line (*I am not good*) will show up in our result line (*I don't do better*).

When I teach people this concept, they often think I'm suggesting that we should believe we are doing a great job no matter what. They think I'm saying that we should approve of all the things we do or say. That we should think we are "good" even when we aren't showing up that way. The truth is, I do think we are all amazing and good no matter what, but it's not that simple. When I teach this concept, I'm actually suggesting that instead of rejecting ourselves, we could just say yes to all of it: Yes to the entire human being that each of us is. Yes to the selfless, loving, giving parts of us, and yes to the selfish, judgmental, greedy parts of us. Yes to acknowledgement. Yes, we are sometimes "bad," we fall short, or we give in to temptation or weakness—and we can love ourselves anyway. Because saying yes to all of it doesn't require that we keep everything. It doesn't mean we can't change. It simply means that shame isn't driving our efforts. Take this new model, for example:

> **Circumstance:** I didn't reach out to help someone I knew was struggling.
>
> **Thought:** Sometimes I don't show up as my best self, and I love me anyway.
>
> **Feeling:** Compassion.
>
> **Action:** I wonder how that friend of mine is doing now. I reach out and ask if there's anything I can do today. I have energy to explore what's really going on for me and why I sometimes avoid serving. I love myself, which allows me to have more space/time/energy/desire to love others.
>
> **Result:** I like the person I'm being.

This thought, "Sometimes I am 'not good' and I love me anyway," never came naturally to me before I understood the model. I never considered it an option. I believed that when I wasn't showing up at my best, I had to either feel terrible and beat myself up or rationalize and justify to decide that my behavior wasn't "bad" after all. For example, I could tell myself that I was just too busy to help that friend or that she probably didn't really need me right now or that I was going to make it up in some way in the future. That would be me thinking, "I didn't do anything wrong here."

But then I learned that I could say yes to all of me.

I could embrace all the parts of me and be willing to allow them without shame, judgment, or self-loathing. I could believe that "I want to be a person who serves others. But if I don't do that service, I am not less valuable. My goodness is the same whether I do it or not. Even when I do something wrong, I am not wrong." When we are willing to embrace all of ourselves, we gain the ability to understand and have some authority over problematic habits and traits. Yes, sometimes I am selfish, I mess things up, and I make a wrong choice even though I know better. Yes. Yes. Yes. I am just as worthy of love, and I am just as valuable on the days when I am not at my best. On other days, I make great choices and am kind, generous, and strong. Yes to me on those days as well.

The next time you find yourself thinking "I'm not a good mom," instead of attempting to believe "I am a great mom," try accepting the truth about what you are noticing. The truth is that you are both a good mom and not a good mom. Some days you are the mom you want to be, and other days you are far from it. You are both good at your calling and not good at it. You are a great wife/sister/friend/employee, and once in a while you are not great in those roles. Embrace the truth of your imperfections and limitations, and stop believing you should be better than you are. When you do, you gain the ability to make the changes you want to make in your behaviors.

Here's the truth, my friends. We are all a complete package—we are full of strength and goodness (the Light of Christ within us),[3] and we are full of struggle because we are human beings with fears and troubles (a part of our mortal experience).[4] This balance within us creates our mortal experience. Our goal is to move away from the fearful side and lean into our loving and trusting side. Sometimes we will do it well, and other times we won't. When we fall short, the way we think about ourselves matters. We can choose self-loathing, or we can choose compassion. Compassion gives us the space to be curious, and curiosity allows us to gain awareness of ourselves. Awareness is the necessary first step to change.

On a daily basis, I hear from people who tell me that my work has helped them find peace and success in their lives and with their goals. People are so kind. They tell me that their kids are listening to the podcast. They tell me that they are different people after learning from me for a while. But on occasion someone writes to tell me that I'm doing it wrong in some way, and they use adjectives like *selfish* and *ignorant*. I used to feel defensive and wanted to justify my behavior or words to them, but I have learned that this is not necessary and not completely honest. If a part of me didn't agree with them, then I would not feel defensive when they describe me this way. So now I say yes to all of it.

Yes, I am selfish sometimes.

I don't mean to be; I try not to be. But sometimes I am. I am also giving and kind at times. I am all those things. And I love all of me.

Yes, I am sometimes ignorant. How could I not be? I can't possibly know everything there is to know, and because I'm human I might try to sound smarter than I am. I'm insecure sometimes, and I am wrong often. And I love me anyway. I am also wise and knowledgeable about some things. Sometimes I am candid, honest, and vulnerable, but other times I pretend out of insecurity and fear.

You nailed it. I am all of these things.

And I will keep showing up in the world as a coach for as long as I find it to be rewarding and as long as someone else, even one person, finds it helpful.

I love all of me.

And I love you, too, my friend.

You can choose to love yourself, you know. You can own all your different qualities, even the ones you'd rather not have, and not make it mean anything terrible. This is not easy to do. Accepting yourself, being compassionate with yourself, and telling the truth about yourself feels scary and challenging at first. But if you're willing to practice acceptance, you'll get better at it. And once you get good at being compassionate with yourself, loving other people is easy.

Yes to all of you.

This changes everything.

The Pride/Shame Continuum

We're taught to beware of pride.[5] We know that in the Book of Mormon, pride led to the fall of the Nephites and Lamanites over and over again, and today we regularly see pride destroy relationships and individuals. I think pride is to blame for the family fights that occur when we're late to church, the current divisive culture of our country, *and* the tragic fashion trends of the late 80s. It's all pride's fault.

Sometimes when I encourage people to embrace all of themselves, they worry about pride, and rightfully so. Pride is no good. But confidence is not the same as pride. Not at all. Pride is not the same as loving all of yourself because pride is based in fear. Pride is a different form of self-rejection than shame, but it is a rejection nonetheless.

Pride, in short, says, "I am better than you," and it gives us all the credit for our success or accomplishments. It presumes that there are levels of human value and that we have some ability to control which level we end up on.[6] None of this is true. When we believe these lies, all our attention goes to avoiding a decline in this perceived "status." C. S. Lewis said, "Pride gets no pleasure out of having something, only out of having more of it than the next man. . . . It is the comparison that makes you proud; the pleasure of being above the rest. Once the element of competition has gone, pride has gone."[7]

In addition, by attributing our value to our accomplishments or characteristics, pride causes us to withdraw from our Heavenly Father, the source of all of our goodness. This disconnection from God and the perceived need to maintain status is how pride sabotages us. Pride is a trap, and it is based in lies about human value and its origin. However, I understand why my clients feel like they're headed for pride when they decide to walk away from shame.

It's because they are.

Sort of.

To get out of the shame trap, it's necessary to head in the *direction* of pride. Shame is equally toxic and damaging, and it is also based in lies. To get out of shame, we must head away from "something is wrong with me" and toward "I am complete." I find it helpful to put pride and shame on opposite ends of a continuum. Either end of the continuum is based in fear and lies and will not serve us. Neither pride nor shame is true confidence; they both deny the equal worth of all humans, and they fail to attribute our worth to our Heavenly Parents.

In the middle of shame and pride is confidence. Confidence is based in love and truth, and it's where we want to land. It says, "I am amazing. So are you. Equally so. And neither of us had anything to do with our value. We can't change it. We can't damage it or increase it, and we don't need to. We're all phenomenal creatures who are infinitely and divinely loved, and there's nothing we can do about it."

Confidence is not arrogant or conceited. When we are in true confidence we are no longer focused on ourselves, because we recognize there is no need to be. We've said yes to ourselves with appreciation for the things we do well and yes to ourselves with curiosity about the ways in which we are a mess. We don't need to justify our value, so we stop putting so much focus on ourselves. If you notice that you have a high percentage of self-focused thoughts, then you are likely on either side of the continuum, closer to shame or pride rather than in the middle where confidence lives.

If you're beating yourself up and telling yourself you shouldn't be in the camp of shame or pride (and you are), then I give you permission to stop it right now. If I thought that beating yourself up would bring you back to confidence, then I might encourage it—but I promise you it does not work. It sends you straight to shame. Please remember that part of our human condition is to question our value and compare ourselves to others. It's human to slide up and down on the continuum, but our goal is to stay as close to the middle for as much of the time as we can.

To help you stay in the middle, let's remember that shame, pride, and confidence are all emotions—feelings that we feel in our bodies. Shame feels terrible. Pride feels dirty. Confidence feels peaceful.

And what do we know about emotions?

Say it with me: They are created by our thoughts.

Let's take a look at some thoughts that will likely generate each emotion. Becoming aware of these thoughts will help you catch yourself when you're believing a shame or pride lie so that you can redirect yourself to a confidence thought.

Shame thoughts:
I'm not as good as she is.
I shouldn't have done that.
I'm not loveable.
I'm not valuable enough.
I can't do it.
I'm not that kind of person.
I'll never get it.
I know better.
Something is wrong with me.
I'm weak.
I'm a mess.

Pride thoughts:
That doesn't apply to me.
My way is the right way.
I do it better.
They should listen to me.
I've arrived.
He shouldn't act like that.

I would never do that (so they shouldn't either).
I already know this.

Confidence thoughts:
I appreciate me.
I love me.
I love me anyway.
I am proud of me for doing that.
She is amazing.
He is fascinating.
There I go again, being a human.
Yes to all of me.
Yes to all of him.
She might be right.
I could be wrong.
Tell me more.

Notice that the shame-filled and pride-filled thoughts shut us down. They prevent us from learning, exploring, moving forward, or putting ourselves out into the world. They disconnect us from other people. They keep us stagnant and create a wall around us, each for different reasons. Confidence-filled thoughts do the opposite. They open us up. They are filled with humility. They allow us to learn, grow, contribute, and connect. Confidence-filled thoughts not only create all of these amazing results for us but also allow us to feel the best feeling on the planet: love. Love for ourselves. Love for others. Love for our Creator.

I am a confident mother, but I didn't used to be. I used to be a confused, insecure, shame-filled mother, and the reason I am a confident mother today is because, once again, I discovered I was wrong about what I believed. I always thought that I wanted to be a *good* mother. As a young girl I imagined how miraculous it would be to have little ones to hold, to bake cookies with, and to tell stories to. I wanted to be loving, patient, and attentive. It was going to be amazing. When my first child was born it *was* amazing at first. I loved him so much it almost hurt my heart. It felt like that much love couldn't be contained in a human body, and I thought I might explode. I desperately wanted to be a good mother to this sweet, tiny boy.

As he grew and more children arrived in our family, I discovered that being a mother is harder than I ever expected. It pushed me in all the ways humans can be pushed at one time, which is to say I was physically, mentally, and emotionally exhausted all the time. Motherhood didn't feel like the fairy tale I had imagined as a child, and I was sure this was my fault. These sweet, innocent children weren't to blame. It was me. I didn't know how to be a mother. I was missing some key motherly traits that many women seemed to have. I just needed to get better at being a mother—that was surely the problem. And then, in my attempts to be a good mother I noticed all the ways in which I was falling short. There were many.

As I mentioned earlier, my oldest child, Isaac, has never been very social. He prefers to stay home. He usually declines invitations to birthday parties and other events, and when you constantly decline invites you stop getting invited after a while. I often worried that he was missing out on the social interaction he needed developmentally or that he was going to feel left out. This worry kept my mama heart on edge, so I was thrilled when Isaac was a first-grader and a boy in his class invited him to a birthday party at an indoor trampoline park. Isaac loved that place, and he told me, to my surprise, that he couldn't wait to go to this party next week. I happily tucked the invitation in the junk drawer and told him that of course he could go.

Exactly seventeen days later I opened up the junk drawer to look for some missing item and my heart sank all the way to the pit of my stomach when I saw that invitation sitting there. It sort of waved at me and said, "Um, hello . . . remember me?" No. No, this can't be. It can't be that I forgot to take my son to the one social event that he had not only agreed to but was really looking forward to. Am I *that* mother? Are you kidding me?

I broke the news to Isaac, whose disappointed face was the dagger in my already broken heart. Then, as usual, I commenced with the self-loathing. I told myself that I had no excuse and that my child, who is already struggling, had this one opportunity and it could have been the one that changed things for him. He was probably going to meet a best friend there and start wanting to hang out with kids and be mentally and emotionally healthier as a result. Now that chance is gone, and it's my fault. Now he's in pain instead, and it's all my fault.

I desperately wanted to be a better mother—to get it together and be more patient, organized, and happy. I tried hard to have those qualities and to get myself to do everything right, but it felt like the task became more challenging the harder I tried. I thought that Heavenly Father had made some sort of mothering-related error when He created me or that I was somehow missing critical information and just needed to find it.

But I was wrong.

I didn't need to be a better mom; I needed to be a *confident* mom. I needed to understand my worth, value, and completeness. I didn't need to do anything other than stop beating myself up and say yes to all of me.

I later came to see this truth by examining myself using the model. Slowly but surely I went to work trying on this strange new way of thinking about myself. I tried on the idea that I am supposed to be *both* a good mother *and* a bad mother because I am a human mother, not a robot mother. I will sometimes do a great job. I will be kind and patient and organized, as I want to be. But other times I will not do as well. I may even snap at or resent my children, or even forget about dream birthday parties they wanted to attend. And then I have a choice to make: either feel terrible for making my children feel terrible or choose compassion and curiosity for myself. Two models. Two different results.

Model 1

Circumstance: I forgot to take Isaac to the party.

Thought: I am a terrible mom, and I should be better.

Feeling: Ashamed.

Action: I spin in negativity. I push others away and myself away. I snap and yell at my family more.

Result: I disconnect from my family and myself, continuing to act like what I think is a bad mother.

Model 2

Circumstance: I forgot to take Isaac to the party.

Thought: Sometimes I fall short, and that's OK.

Feeling: Compassion.

Action: I apologize to Isaac, and I help him process his feelings of disappointment. I make space for myself to process disappointment. I pray for guidance and assistance to help me be better than I could be on my own. I move through this experience and use it to learn about this brilliant invention called a *calendar*.

Result: I remain connected with my family and myself, and we are all OK.

I worked through several versions of Model 2 as I became a confident mother. The circumstances changed, but they consistently included either a mistake I'd made unknowingly or a mistake I'd made as a result of my own weakness. But now the thought was always a version of "I'm OK. I'm good. I don't need to be a better mother than I already am." My brain wanted to go back to Model 1. It wanted me to think I was letting myself off the hook or justifying bad behavior if I stayed with Model 2. This is what Satan wanted me to believe. He wants all of us to stay in Model 1. To convince us to stay in shame, Satan uses the commandments, the council from our Church leaders, and the advice in parenting books to perpetuate the problem. He takes these tools, all of which can be helpful when used correctly, and encourages us to use them against ourselves. But if we take a look at every line of Model 1, from circumstance to result, we won't fall for Satan's lies.

I didn't need to be a better mom; I just had to embrace all of me. The good *and* the bad. The weak *and* the strong. As women we have expectations of ourselves that no human could possibly meet, especially when it comes to our kids. Our children are precious and they matter, and the idea that we might make a mistake when talking with them, raising them, or trying to love them is unacceptable. I get it, but the truth is that we *will* make mistakes. We are human mothers. If Heavenly Father wanted children to come to earth and be free from challenges caused by their mothers' mistakes, then He would have created robot mothers who do everything perfectly every time. But He didn't. He created all of us. With strengths and weaknesses. Faith and fear. Light and dark.

Now, I'm going to share a secret with you—not a secret as in *Don't tell anyone* but a secret as in *Keep this in a closed box* if you're deep in Model 1. When you're ready, you can open the box and discover that when you fully embrace Model 2, when you understand that you don't need to be a better mother but instead believe that you already are a good mother, something miraculous happens. You *do* become a better mother. You won't be a perfect mother; you'll still be a human mother. But when you aren't living under a cloud of guilt and shame, it's easier to deal with a toddler tantrum without having a tantrum yourself. And when you embrace the fact that you are a human who messes up but knows how to love herself anyway, then you understand your teenagers better when they mess up, and you can teach them to love themselves anyway. When you are a confident mother, you enjoy so much more the tasks associated with this part of your life. The heaviness becomes less significant and you live in more lightness. The seriousness becomes more optional and instead you choose fun. The self-judgment is diminished and therefore the judgment of others isn't dominant either.

In the end, what you think really does become your result. Like magic.

Today Isaac, now a high school freshman, doesn't remember that first-grade birthday party he missed, but I know the memory is logged in his subconscious as a sidenote that says, "Mom isn't good at remembering things, so we need to do it ourselves if it matters." I know this because when something important is coming up he reminds me often and tracks it in his own calendar. Maybe this is a good thing. But more importantly, Isaac and I have a special bond today. We both love donuts while the rest of the family favors ice cream. We both prefer peace and quiet over noise and chaos. And we both have a good time with one another whether we're someplace extravagant like Disneyland or someplace ordinary such as on a bike ride in our neighborhood.

But before I did the work to embrace myself as a mother, I pushed my children away. I had to. They were reminders of the things I was failing at, and I couldn't tolerate the pain of it all. I don't believe that today I would have the same bond with Isaac and the rest my children if I hadn't made the decision to be a confident mother. To embrace the fact that I am a good mother and a bad mother. And nothing has gone wrong.

Confidence is the peace we all seek. It's the peace most of us get only in fleeting moments. But you have the ability to feel confidence more often if you choose to pay attention to your beliefs about yourself. This work is worth doing. Loving yourself gives you the capacity to love other people and circumstances even more. Without this foundation of internal self-love, you will struggle to love outside of yourself because we all have a need to protect ourselves first.

Jesus Christ is our perfect example of self-love. During His earthly ministry, He understood His worth. He knew that He was the literal Son of God. He knew that He was here on earth to do an important work. He knew that other people's judgments of Him did not mean anything about His value, and He did not allow even their hatred of Him to cause Him to doubt Himself or His worth. He knew that these people just didn't understand. That they were coming from their own fears and doubts, and He didn't use this as a reason not to love them. In Doctrine and Covenants 45:52 Christ proclaims, "Then shall they know that I am the Lord; for I will say unto them: These wounds are the wounds with which I was wounded in the house of my friends. I am he who was lifted up. I am Jesus that was crucified. I am the Son of God."

In this life, we will never be as perfect at embracing ourselves as Christ is. It's OK if you notice yourself sliding between shame and pride on the continuum. When you understand the truth, which is that your brain is just doing what human brains do and that you can always remind yourself of your value (and that of every other person on the planet), then you will find you can be confident much of the time and rely on the Atonement when you can't.

In our house, when we sing "I am a Child of God and He has sent me here," we modify the next line. Instead of "Has given me an earthly home with parents kind and dear,"[8] we sing, "Has given me an earthly home with parents kind of weird." I like to keep the kids' expectations in check.

My husband and I have three savings accounts for each of our children. One is for a mission. One is for college. And one is for the therapy they will need after being raised by a human mother and father instead of a robot.

---

1. "11 Absolutely Incredible Things Our Body Does Every Day," *Brite Side*, accessed March 11, 2021, https://brightside.me/wonder-curiosities/11-absolutely-incredible-things-our-body-does-every-day-342310/.

2. "Created in the Image of God," *Ensign*, March, 2016, 7, https://www.churchofjesuschrist.org/study/liahona/2016/03/created-in-the-image-of-god?lang=eng.

3. Thomas S. Monson, "Be an Example and a Light," *Ensign*, November 2015, 86–88, https://abn.churchofjesuschrist.org/study/general-conference/2015/10/be-an-example-and-a-light?lang=eng.

4. "The Fall of Adam and Eve," in *Gospel Principles*, 2009, 27–30, https://www.churchofjesuschrist.org/study/manual/gospel-principles/chapter-6-the-fall-of-adam-and-eve?lang=eng.

5. Ezra Taft Benson, "Beware of Pride," *Ensign*, May 1989, https://www.churchofjesuschrist.org/study/general-conference/1989/04/beware-of-pride?lang=eng.

6. Wikipedia, s.v. "Pride," last modified September 8, 2020, 18:05, https://en.wikipedia.org/wiki/Pride.

7. C. S. Lewis, *Mere Christianity* (New York: Macmillan, 1952), 109–110, as quoted in Benson, "Beware of Pride."

8. "I Am a Child of God," *Hymns*, no. 301.

For it must needs be, that there is an opposition in all things. If not so, my firstborn in the wilderness, righteousness could not be brought to pass, neither wickedness, neither holiness nor misery, neither good nor bad. Wherefore, all things must needs be a compound in one; wherefore, if it should be one body it must needs remain as dead, having no life neither death, nor corruption nor incorruption, happiness nor misery, neither sense nor insensibility.

2 Nephi 2:11

11. OPPOSITION IN ALL THINGS

The 50/50 Experience

The 50/50 experience is one of the concepts I learned in coach training that I use with my clients today. Now, I must warn you that when I teach it people often don't like this concept. They want to negotiate with me on the percentages. They want me to be wrong. And do you know what I tell them?

OK.

Maybe I'm wrong here as well.

But looking at life as a 50/50 experience has created peace for me and for many I've taught the concept to since I learned it from my teacher.[1] So before you discount it, consider that I could be right, and that if I am right and we use this tool correctly, we can have the most amazing, happy, and peaceful life possible. I believe that a 50/50 life is exactly what we want, even though we think we want an 80/20 or 99/1 life.

Here's how the concept works: 50/50 represents our emotions. Half of the time we will feel some version of happiness—love, confidence, peace, contentment, surprise, inspiration, joy, and so on. Half the time, we will live in this camp. To simplify, I'll call it happiness, but remember that it comes in many variations and intensities. The other half of the time (you guessed it) we will feel some version of bad—frustration, boredom, anxiety, stress, overwhelm, worry, fear, loneliness, self-pity, confusion, and so on. And half the time we will live in this camp.

As we should.

As we're supposed to.

As is the complete human experience.

When I learned this concept, I kept thinking about 2 Nephi 2:11, the scripture I shared at the start of this chapter. The verse teaches that there is opposition in all things. The idea that if there is opposition in all things, there would be opposition within us rang true to me. In this verse, Lehi, speaking to his son Jacob, even includes human emotions in his description of this truth. So why do we not want to hear this concept? Why does it feel like bad news?

Because we don't understand the beauty of it.

I still don't completely understand the beauty of it, but I want to offer you some examples of how pondering this truth has increased my happiness and and that of many of my clients. Relaxing into the 50/50 experience of life creates *more* happiness than shooting for 80 percent positive and 20 percent negative, and here's why.

When we feel the negative emotions created by our negative thoughts, we have a few choices. First, we can change the thought to a positive one and feel something more positive. This is a good option at times. If my thought is, "I don't like her," and I feel disdain, then changing it to "I love her" and feeling love is a great way to go. But there are many things that we actually want to think and feel negative thoughts and emotions about. If you're asking why in the world would anyone want to feel a negative emotion, then consider some of these thoughts that might not feel good in some circumstances but that we want to keep anyway:

I miss him.

I wish she wouldn't have chosen that.

I regret that I did that.

It's unfortunate that people die young.

It's terrible when people are violent.

People shouldn't take advantage of other people (but they sometimes do).

Children are being hurt every day, and I wish they weren't.

Obviously, we could go on, but I think you get the point. Every one of these thoughts creates a feeling that we would describe as negative. Yet these are all thoughts that I choose to think occasionally. I don't want to never miss loved ones. I don't want to never feel regret when I do something that doesn't align with my values. I don't want to think that violence and mistreatment of others is not a big deal. I want to think that some things in the world are unjust and feel bad as a result of this thought, because the reality is that unjust things do happen.

In other cases, I'd like to change a thought, but I'm just not able to do it, at least not immediately. We are humans with human brains. Our brains come up with some fascinating ideas about what we, the people around us, and our lives should be like. When we argue with reality, we create negative emotions for ourselves. Take for example this model, which was a reality for me earlier this week:

Circumstance: Pink slime on the new ivory-colored upholstered ottoman.

Thought: My kids destroy everything.

Feeling: Frustration.

Action: Snap at children. Complain about it to everyone who will listen. Notice it every time I sit down in the living room. Ruminate about the injustice of it.

Result: I ruin my own experience of my ottoman (and my week).

189

I can work toward changing this thought, but it might not happen immediately when I notice the pink slime on my ivory ottoman. I might need to allow the frustration and understand that slime really has nothing to do with it because I create the frustration with my thinking. But I will more easily access this knowledge by being willing to feel the frustration. When we don't understand the 50/50 experience, we feel even more negative emotion about challenging experiences because we layer on negative thoughts about our negative emotions, as in the following three examples.

1. We feel resentful about how frustrating living with children can be.

Original Thought: My kids destroy everything.

Feeling: Frustration.

Layering Thought: I'm tired of being so frustrated all the time.

Feeling: Resentful.

Now we have resentment *and* frustration.

2. We feel guilty for feeling resentful of our husband going on a business trip while we're home with the kids.

Original Thought: It's not fair that my husband gets to go away for work and I am stuck at home.

Feeling: Resentful.

Layering Thought: I know it's part of his job, and I love my kids. I shouldn't feel this way.

Feeling: Guilt.

Now we have guilt *and* resentment.

3. We feel ashamed that we are irritated with the lady who is serving with us in our Church calling.

Original Thought: She is doing it wrong.

Feeling: Irritated.

Layering Thought: I shouldn't be judging her like this.

Feeling: Ashamed.

Now we feel ashamed *and* irritated.

Rejecting the original thought or the primary experience causes us to layer on more negative emotions, so now rather than 50/50 we are starting to create a 40/60 or other imbalance in favor of the negative. Before we know it, our lives feel difficult. Overwhelming. Stressful. Hard. We can return to the 50/50 balance that allows for maximum happiness by relaxing into the primary negative emotion and knowing that this is how it feels to be a human trying her best but sometimes falling short or downright messing it all up.

Embracing and allowing the primary negative experience creates openness. This openness allows you first to process the original emotion without resisting it or layering it, and second to gain leverage over yourself and your brain. Openness comes from choosing what I call a 50/50 thought to add to your original thought/feeling. It looks something like this:

Example 1

Original Thought: My kids destroy everything.

Feeling: Frustration.

50/50 Thought: This (frustration) is what it's like to be a mom sometimes, and I'm all in.

Feeling: Openness.

Now I'm open to the frustration and can process it and understand my role in creating it. The feeling is not prolonged, and I don't spend much time beating myself up or making my life harder. I roll with the negative and know that the human experience is 50/50.

Example 2

Original Thought: It's not fair that my husband gets to go away for work and I am stuck at home.

Feeling: Resentful.

50/50 Thought: There I go being a human again.

Feeling: Openness.

When I'm open, I allow resentment and relax into it. I understand that the feeling is based in fear and lies and that I don't have to hang on to it. I also know that I don't have to layer resentment with guilt or let it drive my actions. Being a stay-at-home mom is for sure 50/50, and so is being a working dad.

Example 3

Original Thought: She is doing it wrong.

Feeling: Irritated.

50/50 Thought: It's interesting that I keep choosing that thought.

Feeling: Openness.

I like to get curious about why I keep going to thoughts that I know aren't serving me. When I am curious and open like this I learn so much about myself and the world. But to be curious about my thinking I have to be compassionate with myself. I begin by not judging myself so I can gain awareness about why I'm judging others and then ultimately work to minimize that judgment.

Earlier in this chapter I said that truly believing in Lehi's teachings about opposition, including opposition within us, leads to the best-feeling life possible. I've seen this to be true for myself and for thousands of clients. And when I say that the 50/50 experience is the best, I don't mean "that's as good as it gets, so don't try for more"; I mean "This *is* exactly how I want to feel." Because without the contrast we can't experience the positive as fully as we can otherwise.

Positive emotion is like a drink of cold water. We can take a sip when we don't want it because the doctor told us to stay hydrated for optimal health, and we'll experience the water one way. Or we can take a drink when we are thirsty and hot, and that experience will be entirely different. Negative emotions cause the thirst that allows us to fully experience happiness. When you understand more about emotions the opposition within us becomes less scary. Let's take a closer look at how.

The Willingness to Feel

My twelve-year-old daughter, Macy, loves to dance. She has been taking dance classes for only a couple of years, but when she decides to pursue something she goes all in. Because her teachers have emphasized the importance of the ability to do the splits on either leg, for the past year Macy has spent nearly an hour each day stretching. She can now do a full standing split, whereas I am just trying to sit crisscross on the floor without pulling something in my groin. It's incredible.

Macy's ability to do the splits is a result of her time and dedication; it's also a result of her willingness to feel both physical and emotional pain. Physical pain as she gently pushes her muscles to expand in ways they are not used to. Emotional pain as she heads down to the basement to stretch, even though she doesn't feel like it. Commitment is a feeling we all think we want, but it actually doesn't feel very good. If there's nothing to push against, then commitment isn't necessary. Macy's continued willingness to feel all of this pain is the reason why she can do the splits today.

And guess what?

Commitment is the way to success in a standing split, as it is the way to success in every area of life. Your willingness to feel any and all emotions, even the negative ones, will be the determining factor in whether you reach your goals.

Do you want to be more consistent in your parenting? Awesome. What do you think that requires? This week I coached a woman named Sylvia who told me that she is worried about how much time her kids spend on screens. She thinks that the three hours per day they spend is too long because that's what she's been told by doctors, magazine articles, and friends. I asked her why then, if she doesn't want her kids spending three hours a day on screens, is she allowing it, and her clever brain tried to be confused. She told me that she just wasn't sure whether it is a problem because her kids seem fine. Plus, it's convenient to allow the screen time because it keeps the kids occupied so she can get things done. I asked her why she doesn't just ignore the experts and her friends, and she said that she genuinely believes it could be detrimental for her kids in the long run.

Next I told Sylvia what she probably didn't want to hear. I pointed out that her problem is that she is unwilling to feel negative emotions; that is the reason she isn't being the mom she wants to be. When Sylvia creates a plan to monitor screen time and then enforces her policies, she experiences negative emotion. She has overwhelm figuring out the plan, stress about the kids being upset, and frustration when they aren't occupied and she can't get things done. If she were willing to be overwhelmed, stressed, and frustrated, she would be able to be the mom she wants to be.

Similar examples exist with every goal a person might set. Want to grow a successful business? Great. This goal requires that you be willing to feel overwhelm, disappointment, impatience, fear, and frustration. Want to get a college degree? It will cost time and money, but it will also cost stress, boredom, confusion, and determination. Planning to serve a mission? Make sure you're good at feeling rejection, loneliness, homesickness, boredom, and anxiety.

But cheer up, friend. These emotions are the negative 50 percent—don't forget about the positive 50 percent of each of these goals and experiences. This is opposition in all things. Being a mom enables you to experience an abundance of love, connection, pride, joy, amusement, and peace. Running a business allows for success, growth, fascination, accomplishment, and appreciation. Earning a college degree can bring confidence, progression, enlightenment, accomplishment, and success. And serving a mission? One reason this experience is so life-changing is the contrast of emotions missionaries feel. The negative ones are pretty tough to deal with, but the positive ones are amazing. Love, connection, inspiration, revelation, peace, trust, and faith.

Are you in?

Heavenly Father created us, and He created our bodies. Emotions are just the sensations we experience in our bodies when our internal organs release chemicals and hormones.[2] Nothing is wrong when we feel fear in the way the Lord designed us to feel it. Our bodies are simply trying to guide us in the way that our (sometimes confused) brain thinks is best for our survival. When you recognize that there is nothing wrong when you feel "bad" and you learn how to feel all of your feelings, then you become unstoppable.

Truly.

If negative emotions are required for success, then getting good at negative emotions is useful, right? Right.

So how do we get good at them?

The same way we get good at anything—practice. I am constantly striving to get better at feeling my feelings, and fortunately or unfortunately, life gives all of us countless chances to do this.

Several years ago my husband and I relocated our family to the Sacramento area from Southern California, where we'd lived for the first eight years of our marriage. Being new in the ward, Jake and I had been invited to speak in sacrament meeting. We had completely different reactions to this invitation. I enjoy speaking in public. I know this is weird, and I sometimes think my love of public speaking is my way of compensating for years of never feeling heard by peers I didn't fit in with. Regardless, I was confident that I could deliver on this task. Besides, you can't get kicked out of the Church for giving a subpar talk—it's not like you're going to get fired. All of this is to say that I did not put adequate time and attention into preparing my talk, while my husband spent endless hours poring over his preparations.

Jake was nervous. He gets anxious about speaking in public like a normal, emotionally stable person does. He researches his subject and paces out his talk and types it up on his computer. It's not that I never prepare well for a speaking assignment, but on this occasion I was in the thick of dance recitals, grocery shopping, and a million other things, and my talk didn't get the attention it deserved. I wasn't worried because I had an outline of ideas that included scripture references and quotes from General Authorities. Plenty of material.

For several days leading up to our assigned speaking day, and especially the morning of, Jake was on edge. We somehow managed to get the kids dressed, out the door, and settled in the chapel. When it was time, a member of the bishopric announced the program, which would consist of two youth speakers, myself, and then Jake. When it was my turn, I stood up and shared my message, and people seemed to be attentive. I felt the Spirit and I could see the congregation engaged with what I was saying, and I was in my zone. Until I finally glanced up at the clock and thought that perhaps the clock was broken? Because according to the clock I was way over time. I was not only past my projected end time but was nearing the end of Jake's time as well.

My heart climbed all the way up into my throat and I fumbled through a quick wrap-up and sat down. And then the bishopric member stood up and said the words that made my face turn the brightest shade of red it's ever been: "We're so grateful for Sister Moore's message today, and in the interest of time we are going to ask Brother Moore to postpone his talk for another Sunday and conclude our meeting now." This was my model:

> **Circumstance:** I took up all the time for our sacrament meeting talks.
>
> **Thought:** I am ridiculous and now everyone in my new ward knows it!
>
> **Feeling:** Humiliated.
>
> **Action:** Spin in shame in my head. Try to hide, which is hard to do when you're sitting on the pulpit. Leave church right after sacrament meeting and go home to hide. Apologize profusely to Jake, who says it's OK but is clearly unhappy with me. Consider inhaling a lot of food to escape this feeling. Consider moving to a new ward because we couldn't possibly return to this one now.
>
> **Result:** I am being ridiculous and making it even worse for myself.

So, this happened. My head was spinning. I was imagining all the judgmental thoughts everyone must be thinking about me. I was judging me. I was feeling terrible for my husband who had worked so hard to prepare his talk and was now going to have to feel nervous all over again until he gets his turn. But after I left the church building and gained a bit of access to the rational part of my brain, I remembered that I know how to feel my feelings and that today I had a chance to practice it. I remembered that food was not the solution to humiliation and that if I turned to food for escape I would still feel humiliated, but then bloated and guilty as well. So instead of that, I got still with myself for a moment. Now that I was not on full display for the ward the humiliation had shifted to shame. It was dark and hot and powerful. It felt terrible, but I went into my body and felt it. In my head it sounded like this: "This is shame. This is what it's like to be a woman feeling shame. I can feel the shame in my chest. It's incredibly tight. I feel it in my throat too. It's sitting there not really moving. My head feels hot and is throbbing a bit. There it is. I see you, shame. You are here because of sentences in my head (thoughts), but it's OK. You can stay as long as necessary. I'm just going to be a woman feeling shame now. Let's do some shame."

Deep breaths in and out. Relax my body. Open up to shame.

Do you know what happens when you simply allow a feeling? When you get into your body and pay attention to the sensations of those feelings? When you remember that you are a human having a human experience and that nothing has gone wrong? The feeling washes through you, maybe many times, but it gets weaker every time.

When I was a child, my family spent many summers at Lake Coeur d'Alene in Idaho. We kids loved it when a boat would speed past the beach because boats created waves. Those waves would splash onto the beach one at a time, getting weaker with each wave until the lake was still again or another boat came along. When we allow ourselves to feel them, emotions do this in our bodies. A thought comes along like a boat creating waves of emotion, but our bodies know what to do with these chemical reactions. The reactions get weaker as we acknowledge them and stop sending boat after boat after boat in the form of spinning thoughts. This is a skill we can practice and one that I hope we will teach our children.

Christ said, "Be not afraid, only believe."[3] In this verse, *to believe* means to have faith.[4] I don't think this scripture implies that we shouldn't experience negative feelings like sadness, frustration, overwhelm, or even fear. But we don't have to be afraid of those emotions. With faith we know that through and because of Jesus Christ we can be made whole. And I believe that a whole human experiences a range of feelings on this mortal journey. I understand that there are chemical and hormonal factors that sometimes require medicinal or clinical treatment plans to improve, and I highly recommend seeking professional help when needed. In many cases, though, we are simply experiencing opposition in all things. When we are willing to experience all emotions, and we get still with them, our bodies know what to do. Our minds know what to do. Our hearts know what to do.

This is not to say that we should believe every thought or that feelings are facts. Feelings are only suggestions, and sometimes thoughts should be examined and questioned. But overall, nothing is wrong—even when we're having a shame attack. I don't have the flu when I'm feeling shame; I'm not sick. Often if we say to a friend, "I have a lot of anxiety today," the friend replies with ideas about how to "fix" it, as though we have caught the flu and there is a cure. But anxiety is not the flu. Except in the case of a clinical issue, anxiety is purely an emotion and we, as humans, are meant to feel all emotions. We can do it. But we have to stop running away from them, eating them, numbing them, resisting them, or thinking we can't handle them. We can.

Feeling emotions is a superpower you can develop, and it will allow you to create any result you want in your life.

Maybe I made a terrible first impression in that new ward. I don't know. I do believe my husband was annoyed with me for taking up his time and prolonging his anxiety about his talk. I know now that if I fail to properly prepare for a Church talk, I'm likely to go on too long, so even if I'm not nervous, I need to spend time getting ready. Lesson learned.

I am sorry I made that mistake, but I eventually got to the point where I realized that my value is the same as it would have been had I given the perfect talk with perfect timing. I am both a great speaker and a terrible one. And I am a little better at being embarrassed now than I was before, and this could be highly useful. I want to live a big life, and I am never going to be able to hide all of my shortcomings. The price of sharing my work with others is occasional humiliation and shame, so the more I can practice those emotions the less afraid I will be of them. I know them pretty well at this point. They don't feel great, but I can do them, and if this means I can help more people, then I'm all in.

---

1. Brooke Castillo, "The Contrast of Thoughts," November 2, 2017, episode 188 in *The Life Coach School Podcast*, 21:40, https://thelifecoachschool.com/podcast/188/.

2. "The Neurobiology of Emotion: Neural Systems, the Amygdala, and Fear," http://www.neuroanatomy.wisc.edu/coursebook/neuro5(2).pdf.

3. Mark 5:36.

4. Mark 5:36, footnote *a*: "GR exercise faith."

For the natural man is an enemy to God, and has been from the fall of Adam, and will be, forever and ever, unless he yields to the enticings of the Holy Spirit, and putteth off the natural man and becometh a saint through the atonement of Christ the Lord, and becometh as a child, submissive, meek, humble, patient, full of love, willing to submit to all things which the Lord seeth fit to inflict upon him, even as a child doth submit to his father.

Mosiah 3:19

12. THE NATURAL MAN

That Voice in Your Head

I study quite a few spiritual teachers and thought leaders, and many of them explain that there is a part of us that tends toward self-loathing and fear and that, in many cases, it does not represent our true nature. Often they call this part of us *the ego* after the teachings of Sigmund Freud.[1] As members of The Church of Jesus Christ of Latter-day Saints, we call it the *natural man*. Mosiah 3:19 tells us that the natural man is an enemy to God. I used to be confused by this scripture. How could it be that we, in our natural form, are enemies to God? What I've realized is that *we* are not enemies to God. Instead, the enemy is the natural man, or the ego, and this part of us is necessary for our earthly experience because it separates us from God if we yield to it.

The natural man (or woman) is the part of us that has forgotten our divine heritage, that questions our value or worth, that wants us to compare ourselves and our lives to the people around us, and that seeks validation at every turn. Now listen, I'm making the natural man sound pretty bad, and being an enemy to God is a bad thing, of course. But I want to be clear that this part of us could be a gift from our Heavenly Parents to help us become more like Them.

By now you know I love TV. Currently I don't watch as much of it as I would like to, but one day I'll get my priorities straightened out and fit more of it into my life. So I'm behind when it comes to the countless new series available to stream. But one of the shows I used to love to watch is *What Not to Wear*.

In case you haven't seen the show, it featured Stacy and Clinton, two fashion stylists who would take an unsuspecting woman, who had been nominated by a friend or relative for a head-to-toe makeover, and whoosh her away to New York City. There, this team of stylists taught the woman how to dress to flatter her figure, took her on a five-thousand-dollar shopping spree, and completed her look with fresh hair and make-up. The catch was that she had to bring her entire wardrobe with her (all of which was thrown in a trash can right in front of her). A transformation like this is exciting in and of itself, but the show was fun to watch because Stacy and Clinton were life coaches as well as stylists. I mean, they didn't claim to be life coaches, and they probably wouldn't call themselves that, but they were—sort of. They cared about these women and, throughout the makeover process, would take time to listen to them and get to the root of why they were dressing like a teenaged rebel or a gothic grandma.

What I loved about Stacy and Clinton was that they told these women the truth. It wasn't always what they wanted to hear, but it was the truth, and it was a gift to them in the end. When the client modeled her "before" wardrobe, Stacy would shake her head and say, "Seriously. What part of this *ever* seemed like a good idea to you?" or something along those lines, and the client would wonder what was wrong with the tube top and tie-dyed sweats she loved so much. Lest you think I've jumped to another book entirely, let me bring this back to the natural man.

I like to imagine that "the natural man" part of us has its own voice and is like an old friend who feels the need to give us unsolicited and often unhelpful advice. My own personal "natural man" voice sounds exactly like Stacy London from *What Not to Wear*. She tells me the truth (or what *she* believes is truth, anyway), and she disapproves of many things about me, but she means well.

"That's what you came up with?" she often asks after I finally choose my outfit for the day.

"What's the matter with these people?" is a favorite question of hers, especially when I get a Marco Polo that is twenty minutes long or when my kids complain about having to pick up their rooms again.

"This is ridiculous. Nobody should have to live like this" is one of her favorite sentences.

She flips her long black hair with that signature silver streak and smiles as I do something like load two crying kids into the car, and she tries to convince me that I should feel sorry for myself.

But the Stacy London in my head is not like the real one. The real Stacy London (who I decided is my friend, although she doesn't know it) is doing great work in the world by helping people into better clothes, and better self-images in the process. The one in my head is a bit cynical and critical of me, and of the world around me. She is fearful of rejection, failure, disappointment, embarrassment, judgment, or anything too challenging. She thinks we should buy something new anytime we go into a store. She thinks some people are better than others, and she thinks that we should make sure we never miss out on anything great or fun. And for some reason she thinks life should be fair. She is my natural (wo)man. I love her, but she is misguided.

The natural man is a part of all healthy humans, and we will never shed it entirely in this life.[2] The key to managing it is to not allow the Stacy London in your head to run the show. The key is to notice when this "default setting" we have as humans is actually getting in our way. Know that you have the ability to override it and to choose more intentionally who you want to be or how you want to feel. It is possible to set the natural man aside.

Above the natural man, there is another part of us. It's our spirit in its purest, most loving, and most trusting form. It's often hard to access, but it's available to you. This part of you has a much different voice and believes things like the following:

Everything will work out.

Nothing has gone wrong.

My only job is to love her.

I can do hard things.

Anything is possible.

It's OK for people to be wrong about me.

She doesn't need to be any different than she is.

His only job is to be there for me to love.

I love me, I love you, I love us.

This is going to be fun.

All of these thoughts are available to us. If we put them in models, they produce a great result. But these thoughts can be difficult to get to because of the natural man. We must choose to overcome that part of us if and when we want to feel lighter, happier, more free, and more confident. Every one of these thoughts is believable if you also believe that Jesus Christ personally experienced your suffering. If the Atonement is real, and if His sacrifice means that this life is temporary and that healing and eternal glory are attainable for everyone, then all of the thoughts I've listed here (and more) are true.

It is easier to put aside the natural man when we put our trust in the Lord. When we hear Him and strive to know Him, our trust will increase. We can begin this process by pondering such scriptures as 2 Nephi 9:20–21: "O how great the holiness of our God! For he knoweth all things, and there is not anything save he knows it. And he cometh into the world that he may save all men if they will hearken unto his voice; for behold, he suffereth the pains of all men, yea, the pains of every living creature, both men, women, and children who belong to the family of Adam."

Our work as children of Heavenly Parents is to get good at living in this space of trust and love. This is where They live. Trust and love is Their truth. And if you choose to be wrong about any fearful thoughts you may have, Their truth can be yours as well.

The False-Pleasure Trap

We live in an amazing world.

No, really.

It's extraordinary, this world we live in.

We live in a world where you can watch basically anything you want to on TV at any time without waiting for it to come on or even having to deal with commercials. When I was a kid, you didn't get up from the couch to use the bathroom until the commercial break or you would miss part of *Knight Rider*. But today we just press pause if we need to step out. Amazing.

Did you know, there are places in this wonderful world where you don't even have to go inside the grocery store and walk up and down the aisles collecting your food, then haul it all up front and out to your car on a cold winter day? I live in one of those places. You can just hop online, and a few clicks later your virtual cart is full. Later that day, you get in your car, plug in your phone, and turn on your favorite music. You drive to the store parking lot and call to let them know you've arrived (because we can't be bothered to get out in the cold), and someone brings your groceries out and loads them into the back of your car while you scroll Instagram on your phone.

Magic, I tell ya.

I love the world we live in.

But sometimes our efforts to make the world more enjoyable, more pleasurable, less painful, and less challenging result in some traps that we fall into and then get stuck. I call them false-pleasure traps, and we get caught in them because the natural man is tough to overcome, especially given all the temptations that speak to this part of us.

Before you start thinking I'm about to vilify some of the most fantastic parts of our world, let me say that certain things I'm going to discuss are not problems for many people. If you can enjoy these pleasures in moderation and there is no downside to doing so, then I'm all in. The problem is that the natural man doesn't like moderation, and most people aren't satisfied with "some" when more is an option.

I don't believe in telling you what you should or shouldn't do. I am a fan of empowering you with knowledge about what's happening in your brain so that you have more authority over yourself—especially the part of you that is the natural man. When you understand what's going on in your brain, you stop being at the effect of the thoughts driving unhealthy desires. And you gain the ability to change these thoughts. If you don't experience negative consequences from any of these false pleasures, then good on you. Skip to the next chapter. But if you have struggled at some point with a false pleasure that is preventing you from reaching your potential, then let's take a look at what's really happening.

A *false pleasure* is a concentrated pleasure that is typically artificial and might speak to one of our natural, healthy desires but in a more extreme and often unhealthy way. There are many examples in our world today, including social media (concentrated connection), alcohol (concentrated relief from emotions), refined sugar (concentrated food), pornography (concentrated sex), video games (concentrated strategizing/winning), sodas and energy drinks (concentrated energy), drugs (concentrated brain manipulation), and shopping (concentrated gathering of supplies). So, as you can see, not all of these things are problematic in and of themselves, but they can all cause problems if used in excess, and some are best to avoid altogether.

To illustrate what happens in our brains when we indulge in false pleasures, I like to use overeating and pornography as examples. Many people think that because viewing pornography has moral implications and overeating does not, different impulses are driving the behaviors. But that is not the case. The brain loop driving these actions is the same. The consequences and negative effects of these two false pleasures are different, but the root cause of indulging in them is the same. It's the false-pleasure trap. I also like to use these two topics as examples because most people have struggled with at least one of them, and the topics can bring up significant emotion for people. And that's not to say I'm trying to stir up drama.

I'm not.

In fact, the opposite is true.

I want to show you that the same brain loop keeps people stuck with an overeating problem *or* with a pornography problem. It's not because something is wrong with them. Nothing is. It's not because they are bad people. They're not. When we find ourselves over-desiring something that creates problems for us in other ways, we simply have wired our brains, through repeatedly rewarding it, to desire that false pleasure.

Our brains are incredible. They are designed to seek things that will contribute to our survival and avoid things that might not.[3] The only problem is that our brains are confused by the synthetic conveniences and instant false gratification we expose them to. Every time we engage with a concentrated pleasure, our brain takes note.

That was amazing.

That will keep us alive forever.

We should do that as much as possible.

Let's first take a look at overeating. If we all kept eating smashed carrots and milk like we did as babies, and we never tried chocolate cake, chips with guacamole, or fettuccine alfredo, we would not have many of the health problems we have today. We aren't born wanting to snack on chocolate chips all day. We learn that. We learn it by eating chocolate chips and getting the concentrated hit of dopamine they give us. Our clever brains take note and later tell us (plead with us, in fact) that we should do it again. Every time we answer that call, we reinforce this "thought error" in the brain.

Circumstance: Chocolate chips.

Thought: I want to eat those.

Feeling: Desire.

Action: I eat some or all of them and get a large dopamine release in the brain.

Result: My brain learns that eating chocolate chips feels amazing, and now I want them even more.

See how we make the thought "I want to eat those" even stronger with this model? That's why I call this type of model a brain loop—we loop around in the problem, and it's challenging to break out of. But this is a natural-man problem. This is not coming from your spirit, your highest, most trusting, wise self. Your higher self understands that a steady diet of chocolate chips and ice cream will not create your best outcome. You know what your body truly wants and needs to remain healthy and strong. We like to pretend that it's confusing and overwhelming to make good choices about nutrition, but the reality is that it is very simple. While the diet industry and the countless opinions about what you should or shouldn't eat and think about this topic are far from simple, you can simply pick a plan you feel good about. It's sticking to the plan that is the difficult part. The challenge is to overcome the natural man, the lower brain that has been misinformed and prefers an immediate, sure form of pleasure over a potential longer-term payoff.

Watching pornography has the same effect. Let's take a look.

Circumstance: Pornography.
Thought: I want to watch it.
Feeling: Desire.
Action: I watch pornography and get a large dopamine release in the brain.
Result: My brain learns that watching pornography feels amazing, and now I want to watch it even more.

Food is a good thing. It is necessary for our survival as a species. Sex is also a good thing. It too is necessary for our species to survive and thrive not only because of the reproductive component but also because of the way it creates connection and bonds us. Either one in concentrated amounts is problematic and diminishes our ability to survive and thrive. Too much food makes us sick in various ways. Pornography distorts our ability to create an intimate connection through sex and creates problems in relationships.[4] But I have the utmost compassion and respect for anyone who is stuck in a false-pleasure trap. Telling someone to "stop doing it" is an oversimplified response to a complicated natural-man problem.

So, what is the answer, then? How do we break free from brain loops? How do we overcome the natural man? And why should we? With some of these false pleasures, the problems they create are obvious and immediate, and they are matters of moral and spiritual importance. With other false pleasures, we see long-term negative consequences or inconveniences, like feeling bloated, that we may say don't matter that much. But I believe that we distance ourselves from God and the Spirit when we stay stuck in the false-pleasure trap, no matter what the false pleasure may be.

The Spirit speaks to us in a still, small voice. It's subtle, and it lives on a certain frequency. In other words, if I'm tuning my radio (the emotions I'm living from)[5] to the frequencies of guilt, shame, judgment, stress, frustration, or anger, then I likely won't hear the Spirit because the Spirit doesn't reside at those frequencies. The Spirit resides where there is peace, love, inspiration, determination, and faith. When we tune in to that frequency and make our best effort to stay there, we will experience the results listed in Galatians 5:22–23: "The fruit of the Spirit is love, joy, peace, longsuffering, gentleness, goodness, faith, meekness, temperance." False pleasure doesn't feel like any of those good things. Not for more than a few seconds, anyway.

Have you noticed that eating chocolate cake is not the same as feeling love? There is the momentary burst of pleasure from the first bites, but then after we've eaten more than enough to be satisfied, we start to go numb. We stop feeling anything. This numbness blocks negative emotion, so the cake becomes a welcome escape, but the escape itself is the problem. The Spirit cannot reside with us as we escape from ourselves. It is only by being present with ourselves, even through discomfort, that we learn to understand the Spirit, make peace with it, and connect with God through it.

Our willingness to remain in frustration (or any other negative emotion) helps us access the emotion's root cause and allows us to receive the blessings of the Atonement. I genuinely believe that if we are willing to feel negative emotions, the Lord will guide us to overcome them. I also believe that even though part of our brain is wired to crave false pleasure, we have the ability to rewire it for something more useful. The rewiring begins with understanding your current thinking and then questioning your thoughts. Then you must be willing to be uncomfortable. Just experience the discomfort. Don't answer it, don't try to get rid of it, just be with it. This process is what I call interrupting your model, and it looks like this:

Circumstance: Pornography.
Thought: I should watch it.

At this point I can interrupt my model by noticing my thought. It might sound like this:

I don't actually want to watch pornography. My brain is just confused. It thinks it is very important to my survival. What I want is to not want to watch it. If I watch it I'll keep wanting to do so in the future. If I don't watch it, eventually I won't want to so much.

Interrupting your model doesn't mean you won't have the feeling of unanswered desire. You will, and it will feel uncomfortable. But you'll have some authority over your emotions. You might also generate some curiosity or commitment with your thoughts. Another way to think about interrupting your model is to do so after you experience the Feeling:

Circumstance: Pornography.
Thought: I should watch it.
Feeling: Desire.

Did you know you can feel desire and not answer it? You won't die. You won't explode. You will be just fine. It took me a long time to trust this, but I've experienced it with food and shopping, and I have watched my clients experience it enough that I feel confident advising you that you can do it too. We interrupt a model here at the feeling line by allowing the desire. I mean really allowing it. We don't resist it or push against it. We don't use willpower. We are actually present in our bodies and discover what it's like to be a human who is experiencing unanswered desire.

Unanswered desire feels hollow. It sometimes feels tight in the throat or chest. It feels like a pulling downward toward your abdomen. It feels a bit uncomfortable, and that's all. It's not that big of a deal. When you take a deep breath and allow yourself to experience this emotion, you'll find that feeling desire without answering it is a skill you can develop. It's a highly useful skill, given the world we live in and our tendency to fall into the false-pleasure trap. When you're willing to feel unanswered desire, you gain authority over it. You learn that it isn't a big deal. And every time you allow desire without answering it, you begin rewiring your brain to not crave it so much.

Sometimes as you do this work, the natural man will win out, and you will give in to the desire. After this happens, the way you address yourself matters tremendously. When we beat ourselves up with thoughts like, *I'm so weak, I will never overcome this, I can't believe I did that, I am a terrible person,* we create even more problems. Thoughts like this actually make it *harder* to get back on track. This is the way Satan wants us to think. He wants us to believe that something is wrong with us and that we are not good enough to do better. He knows that if we believe those thoughts about ourselves, we will make them true. He understands the model at work within us:

> **Circumstance:** I looked at pornography.
> **Thought:** I am a terrible person.
> **Feeling:** Ashamed.
> **Action:** I want to look at pornography again to escape feeling so awful about myself. I don't want to examine myself, my thoughts, or my actions because I feel ashamed, so I attempt to hide from all of it.
> **Result:** I prove to myself that I'm a terrible person.

Elder Jeffrey R. Holland explained this concept beautifully:

What I now say in no way denies or diminishes any commandment God has ever given us. I believe in His perfection, and I know we are His spiritual sons and daughters with divine potential to become as He is. I also know that, as children of God, we should not demean or vilify ourselves, as if beating up on ourselves is somehow going to make us the person God wants us to become. No! With a willingness to repent and a desire for increased righteousness always in our hearts, I would hope we could pursue personal improvement in a way that doesn't include getting ulcers or anorexia, feeling depressed or demolishing our self-esteem. That is not what the Lord wants for Primary children or anyone else who honestly sings, "I'm trying to be like Jesus."[6]

I know it feels important to criticize yourself. It may seem like you are acknowledging what you believe is right or wrong. But it is neither of those things. Criticizing yourself is toxic. It is a trap. It will keep you stuck and spinning, and I've seen proof of this over and over again. The alternative to self-judgment is compassion, kindness, and curiosity:

> **Circumstance:** I looked at pornography.
> **Thought:** I am a good person, so I must really be struggling to have done that.
> **Feeling:** Curious.
> **Action:** I take a look at what was going on for me that led me down that path.
> **Result:** I gain some awareness and leverage over the root cause of this problem.

Treat yourself kindly. The reason we engage in behaviors that are ultimately harmful is always because we are going through some sort of struggle. We are struggling with fear, self-doubt, overwhelm, or confusion. The answer is not to layer on more hate, judgment, and criticism. The answer is to chip away at fear with love. To chip away at self-pity with self-confidence. To replace shame with curiosity, and judgment with compassion. And we do so by carefully choosing how we will think about ourselves through the process of learning to allow unanswered desire.

I started regularly drinking Diet Coke when I was a junior in high school. I would stop at the 7-Eleven on the way to school every day and get a Super Big Gulp. I needed the caffeine boost after my 6:00 a.m. seminary class, and I soon became hooked on the cold, fizzy buzz of that morning Diet Coke.

Diet Coke was not just my wake-up drink of choice, it became my identity—the kids at school knew me as the girl who drank Diet Coke instead of wine coolers. I continued this habit into college and beyond. A friend who was not a member of the Church once said to me, "You know how you can tell who the cool Mormon girls are? They drink Diet Coke." He was wrong, but I didn't tell him that. I just winked and took a sip of my Big Gulp.

Sometimes people I loved told me that drinking that much Diet Coke was not good for me, and I thanked those people by not answering their calls for a while. Once someone even sent me an article describing a study that showed a correlation between diet soda and cancer in lab rats. "Well, you pump a rat full of enough of anything and you can probably give it cancer," was my reply. I didn't care. I didn't want to hear it. I needed that Diet Coke. I wanted that Diet Coke. It was my friend. It kept me company in my car and in class. It was the perfect companion to some of my other friends like pizza and licorice. I loved Diet Coke. The only problem was that Diet Coke didn't love me back.

After a while I began having extreme blood sugar lows where I became shaky and sweaty and felt that if I didn't eat an entire bag of Skittles right away I might die. Later on, when I developed gestational diabetes during pregnancy and began paying closer attention to my blood sugar levels, I discovered that drinking Diet Coke spikes my blood sugar (resulting in a huge crash later). This is not true for most people, but it is for me. Maybe my body doesn't know the difference between real sugar and artificial sugar. Maybe it is exhausted from the steady diet of Diet Coke and junk food I gave it for so long. It doesn't really matter. What matters is that I know that Diet Coke is not doing me any long-term favors and, in fact, may be creating huge problems that I'd like to avoid down the road.

Now, this isn't a story about how I came to this realization and then got motivated and quit drinking Diet Coke. I wish that were my story, but it's not. The real story is that I quit Diet Coke at least a half-dozen times and then went back to Diet Coke. Allowing unanswered desire is tough. Feeling your feelings is tough. But there is no limit to how many chances you get to rewire a false-pleasure trap. Take as many as you need. The alternative is that we don't try and we create problems in our lives. Trying and failing is better than failing ahead of time by not trying at all.

This is also not a story about how today I never drink Diet Coke and never miss it and my life is better as a result and if I can do it you can drop your bad habit too. That story would be nice but slightly boring; you also might want to punch me in the face for telling it. I still do drink a glass of Diet Coke on occasion, like when eating out. The real story is that I *accidentally* reduced my Diet Coke consumption last year when I started eating differently. Diet Coke with baby carrots is not tasty. Diet Coke with egg whites . . . not amazing. And including Diet Coke in your day when you're also drinking 100 ounces of water is challenging. So, slowly but surely, I broke up with Diet Coke. Physically I felt noticeably better, but emotionally I felt like I had lost my best friend.

I wondered why I felt this low-grade depression, and when I took a look at my thoughts here's what I realized. I used to, most afternoons, take a break from my work day and go to a convenience store where I'd pick up a 44-ounce Diet Coke to nurse for the rest of the day. Since dropping that routine I had been missing my midday escape and my get-through-the-afternoon vice. But it wasn't just the afternoon that felt like a letdown. My mornings did too, and the reason why, the thought I found, is the most shocking and useful information I've learned about myself since changing my food and beverage intake. Without that Diet Coke break I believed I had nothing to look forward to.

Did you *hear* that? I have a beautiful family of four incredible kids, a loving husband, a cat who follows me everywhere, and a dog that my kids play with in the backyard all day. I am educated and have a job I love that allows me to work from home and be my own boss. I live in an amazing neighborhood and have friends and family all around me. I don't have to fear for my or my loved ones' safety. I am healthy and I have a refrigerator and pantry full of fresh food to feed my family. I have clean drinking water from my kitchen faucet, and I never wonder if it's going to work or be safe to drink. Not ever. Heck, I even get to go on a vacation every now and again. And my thought was, "I just don't have anything to look forward to now that I don't drink Diet Coke."

Seriously.

That's where I was. This realization was extremely eye-opening. Do you know what I want the best part of my day to be? Not a diet soda—that's for sure. Without it, though, there was an emptiness in me that lasted for a while. But here's what I've discovered about the empty places within us: they don't feel good, but if we're willing to sit with them for a time, something better is available and waiting to fill that void.

Today I look forward to Skip-Bo, the card game everyone in my family can and will play. We all sit down together and play a game with real cards at an actual table. It feels like magic. We eat snacks, laugh, and smack talk with one another about who is going to win this game of mostly luck. It's beautiful when we play Skip-Bo, and now I see that with more clarity.

I also go for a walk every day—a long walk. On occasion I go with a friend but usually I go alone. My walk has become the time when I get quiet. I listen for promptings from the Lord. I search for inspiration and ideas about my family, my business, and my clients. When I'm on my walk I have time to think. I have space and fresh air, and I can center myself. Now I look forward to that walk instead of a diet soda.

And this isn't to say that the Diet-Coke-shaped hole in my heart is all filled in. I still struggle on occasion. But I'm leaving some space in my heart; I'm not in a rush to fill it up. I want to see what extraordinary things I can discover or create in my life. I'm allowing room for miracles and magic because when it's all filled in with diet soda I don't see the miracles or the magic. They become lost in the chaos of my life, my head, and my heart. I want to be free from the chaos and present for the magic.

I want to continue noticing the simple blessings I take for granted. I want to love my life more. I want to look forward to things that bring true joy instead of substituting joy for false pleasure. But I also want to be present with what's real for me. If I am lacking gratitude and missing the good stuff, then I want to accept that reality so I can examine my thoughts.

I genuinely do not care which foods you choose or how much money you spend. I understand the appeal of video games, and I have zero judgment for someone who is looking at pornography. I simply know that on the other side of these false pleasures is a more extraordinary life. It's a life in which we feel in control of our desires and actions and truly connect with real, live people. We minimize stuff, thereby reducing overwhelm. We seek out real problems and create genuine solutions instead of living in a virtual reality. We feel better in our bodies and have more strength to do what we choose to do. And best of all, we are able to feel the Spirit directing us for good, as Elder Boyd K. Packer taught: "Surely the Word of Wisdom was given so that you may keep the delicate, sensitive, spiritual part of your nature on proper alert. Learn to 'listen' to your feelings. You will be guided and warned and taught and blessed."[7]

The natural man in you won't like it when you begin making these changes in your life. He or she is very good at selling you on all the reasons you should stay in the false-pleasure trap. But you have the ability to make choices. That fear-based voice in your head cannot make you do anything. It can only generate emotions, which is why your emotions feel so strong. But remember that you get to choose what you will do with what poet Mary Oliver calls "your one wild and precious life."[8] How you will spend the next day or hour or minute is your choice.

Is overcoming the natural man hard?

Yes.

But so what?

Let it be hard. We are capable of doing some extremely hard things, and in the end, doing hard things creates an extraordinary life.

---

1. Mark Leary, "What Is Ego, and Why Is It So Involved in My Life?" *Psychology Today*, May 13, 2019, https://www.psychologytoday.com/us/blog/toward-less-egoic-world/201905/what-is-the-ego-and-why-is-it-so-involved-in-my-life.

2. Kendra Cherry, "Ego as the Rational Part of Personality," *Very Well Mind*, https://www.verywellmind.com/what-is-the-ego-2795167.

3. John Medina, "Survival: The Human Brain Evolved, Too," *Brain Rules by John Medina* (blog), accessed September 17, 2020, http://www.brainrules.net/survival.

4. Grant Hilary Brenner, "4 Ways Porn Use Causes Problems," *Psychology Today*, March 5, 2018, https://www.psychologytoday.com/us/blog/experimentations/201803/4-ways-porn-use-causes-problems.

5. "Understanding Emotions," Spacious Therapy, https://spacioustherapy.com/understanding-emotions/.

6. Jeffrey R. Holland, "Be Ye Therefore Perfect—Eventually," *Ensign*, October 2017, https://abn.churchofjesuschrist.org/study/general-conference/2017/10/be-ye-therefore-perfect-eventually?lang=eng.

7. Boyd K. Packer, "The Word of Wisdom: The Principle and the Promises," *Ensign*, April 1996, https://www.churchofjesuschrist.org/study/general-conference/1996/04/the-word-of-wisdom-the-principle-and-the-promises?lang=eng.

8. Mary Oliver, "The Summer Day," in *House of Light* (Boston: Beacon, 1990), 60.

And I said: Lord, how is it done?
And he said unto me: Because of thy
faith in Christ, whom thou hast never
before heard nor seen. And many years
pass away before he shall manifest
himself in the flesh; wherefore, go to,
thy faith hath made thee whole.

Enos 1:7–8

13. FAITH

The Power of Faith

Becoming aware of the fact that we can choose our thoughts and beliefs and that these choices will affect our results has changed me profoundly. I've watched the model operate in my own life and in my clients' lives, and seeing the process play out is truly life changing. Taking accountability for our results brings personal power, which I define as full ownership of our thoughts, feelings, actions, and results. I think that the Lord desires this personal power for all of us because it helps us become more like Him, and as we do so, it helps us have our most ideal experience on earth.

Some thoughts are easy to believe, and we have plenty of evidence that they are true. Many people believe these same thoughts, so we feel supported and it feels safe and easy to keep thinking them. These could be thoughts like, *The sun will rise tomorrow. Babies are precious. Taylor Swift is a magical lyrical-unicorn-genius.*

But then there are thoughts that are less evidence-based or less shared by others. I love trying on these thoughts—thoughts that I have no right to believe, that I have no proof of, and that some might even call naïve, delusional, or unrealistic. I know that the better I get at believing thoughts that my brain has to wrestle with—if they are thoughts that will create results I desire—the more amazing my life becomes. And it turns out that as a member of The Church of Jesus Christ of Latter-day Saints, I am already skilled at believing because I have been taught the power of faith.

Faith.

As in, the ability to believe in something that you cannot see, touch, taste, or otherwise know for certain to be true. Faith is the first principle of the gospel of Jesus Christ.[1] It's what made Enos whole.[2] Believing provable facts and then successfully achieving his goals did not make Enos whole—faith did.

Faith is an extremely important part of the doctrine we believe in. One reason why may be because the Lord knows the power of developing the skill of faith. I think of it as a skill because developing faith can be challenging, but as with any skill, we become better at it with practice. Faith gives us the ability to answer our doubt-filled, natural-man brains with the thought "I just know in my heart this is true, even though I can't prove it."

Jesus Christ is the Son of God and He atoned for our sins. The plan of salvation depends on the Atonement. Following his vision of God the Father and Jesus Christ, Joseph Smith worked to restore the Church of Jesus Christ to the earth. None of these claims can be proven through data collection or scientific research, but God will affirm their truth to us if we ask in faith.

With faith.

To begin developing the skill of faith, we can start small. First, we must choose to at least partially believe these Church doctrines, as we learn in Alma 32:27: "But behold, if ye will awake and arouse your faculties, even to an experiment upon my words, and exercise a particle of faith, yea, even if ye can no more than desire to believe, let this desire work in you, even until ye believe in a manner that ye can give place for a portion of my words." We must at least *want* to believe, and if we do, then the Spirit will testify to us and deepen our understanding and belief.

Our belief will be deepened even though not everyone believes, even though some people will provide evidence to the contrary. We have the capacity to believe in the doctrines, but we must also use our agency. Our Divine Parents sent us to earth and provided tools to help us return to Them, but They held back the hard proof of the plan and even of Their existence so that we would need to exercise our faith if we wanted to follow Them. What a perfect plan.

Faith feels scary sometimes, but when you learn that there is actually nothing to fear at all, then you get better at it. Our human brains prefer the safety of proof, but the beautiful thing about faith is that, by definition, it requires no proof. In fact, we're taught that we must have faith *before* the Lord can reveal the way or provide the blessing.[3] I love what faith requires of us. Faith fits into the model as follows:

Circumstance: Me.

Thought: I want to believe that God exists.

Feeling: Faith.

Action: I open my heart to believing. I pray, study the scriptures, and invite the Spirit into my heart.

Result: I develop a testimony of God.

Faith is the way the Lord works and the way He created us. However, our brains don't like faith, especially when it comes to our temporal goals. When we set out to achieve a goal, our brains think we can't do it unless we already know how, and it's even better if we have a guarantee that we can do "it" or that "it" will work. Often, our lack of belief, or lack of faith, causes us to sabotage our success. If we're operating from doubt and fear, the odds of achieving our goals go down significantly. If we choose faith, however, we end up in a completely different place.

In the Book of Mormon, Nephi demonstrated the power of choosing to believe. When the Lord told him to build a ship, Nephi didn't respond the way I would have responded. I might have said, "But Lord, I don't know how. I've never even built a tiny boat let alone an entire *ship*. So please give me all the directions so I can look them over, and then I'll let you know if I can do this thing you ask."

This is how we respond to our goals in many cases. We want to know exactly how to accomplish something before we give ourselves permission to believe we can do it. We don't want to proceed without some sort of guarantee. Our brains tell us that if we can't see the entire path or find solid proof that we will succeed, then it's dangerous to believe we can accomplish our goal. Because our brains think it's dangerous to be wrong. But what if it's not? What if choosing to believe, even if we are wrong, could be very useful? What if believing is actually the most important part of pursuing a goal? As we pursue goals, faith is the emotion that is extremely useful fuel for our actions.

Nephi chose to believe that he could build a ship with the Lord's help. He had faith and simply asked for assistance in getting started: "And it came to pass that the Lord spake unto me, saying: Thou shalt construct a ship, after the manner which I shall show thee, that I may carry thy people across these waters. And I said: Lord, whither shall I go that I may find ore to molten, that I may make tools to construct the ship after the manner which thou hast shown unto me?"[4]

This was Nephi's model:

Circumstance: The Lord wants me to build a ship.
Thought: I trust that he will show me how.
Feeling: Faith.
Action: I ask him where I should go to start making the proper tools. I get creative about how to solve problems. I access wisdom and creativity. I am open to hearing answers from the Lord
Result: I build a ship.

Now, listen. I don't believe in sitting on the couch chanting affirmations and expecting checks to show up in the mailbox. The Bible tells us that "faith without works is dead."[5] I believe the Lord wants us to show up and work toward our goals. I believe what Pablo Picasso said: "Inspiration exists, but it has to find you working."[6] Even if we have faith, sometimes things don't turn out how we wanted, and certainly not always on our timeline. But our work is more effective when it's fueled by excited anticipation than by discouraged doubt. Because the eye sees what the mind looks for, if we aren't looking for ways to achieve our goals, then opportunities and even blessings from the Lord may go completely unnoticed. Sometimes a miracle can happen. Sometimes when we move forward with faith, doing all we can, we arrive at our goal in a way we never could have predicted. This is the power of faith in our lives.

Is it foolish to believe in things you can't see, touch, or prove? Some people would say so. Is it natural to struggle and feel discomfort to have faith in some things? I think so. But I also believe that learning the skill of faith is a magical, powerful part of our journey and that it will help us to create extraordinary lives. I believe it serves us well to put our faith in good things, to keep believing when challenges come, and to have faith even when everyone around us does not.

I had been a coach for a few years when I decided to change my business model from individual private coaching to group coaching and classes (a program I call Be Bold). I felt that this change would allow me to help more people because I could make coaching more affordable. This new format could also provide more work-life balance so I could be more available to my family. It made sense for me, for my clients, and for the business. I shared my plans for the program with my family and friends, but what I didn't tell them at the time was that I knew that this change would be extraordinary.

Not extraordinary as in, "Look at me and all my success."

But extraordinary as in, "This increased access to coaching will be life-changing for so many people, and those people will become examples of this work. They will then teach their families, and we will all create significant changes in our collective mental/emotional health as a result."

In the Book of Mormon we learn about the two thousand stripling warriors who took up arms to protect their families and won the battle against all odds. We're taught that their success came as a result of their righteousness and their faith in God. And then, in one of my most favorite verses, we find that they were able to have this faith because they piggy-backed on the faith of their mothers. I get goosebumps when I read "We do not doubt our mothers knew it."[7] As mothers and fathers today we have the same opportunity to show our kids the power of being spiritually grounded in the gospel of Jesus Christ. And I would also love for us to show them the power of being mentally and emotionally strengthened and to teach them the power of knowing how to examine their thoughts and choose their emotions.

Most people appreciate the value of strengthening and maintaining physical health. As members of the Church we understand the value of doing the same thing with spiritual health. I would like us to add a third layer of health—mental and emotional. I want us to lead the way for our children. Given the large percentage of our population (including young people) that struggles with depression and anxiety today, I feel called to provide the resources and tools that have helped me and many others.

This was my vision, and I decided to believe in it even though nobody told me I could.

I had faith.

I envisioned the crowds of women who would want to learn these tools, get coached, and work on themselves. I had no business believing that I could find these women or that they would want to learn from me. I did not have a large following or much money to spend on marketing. But I decided to believe in my vision anyway. I pictured these women coming to my coaching calls and being vulnerable, and I imagined them improving their marriages, building their confidence, and pursuing their goals. Nothing I had done in the past would indicate that I could create a program like this, but I decided to believe it anyway because in my heart I knew that my desire was good. I felt the Spirit witness to me that this was a righteous pursuit, and I chose to have faith.

I kept this goal to myself because it was fragile, like a newborn baby. I didn't want to pass it around for everyone to hold and possibly infect with their germs or, in other words, their opinions. Believing in a vision is tough, and I knew that if others tried to tell me it wasn't possible I'd be tempted to believe them, so I kept my vision close to me and nurtured it, cared for it, and helped it grow stronger. It was mine to cuddle and love and nobody else's.

Faith requires effort because you must have an answer for your brain when it says things like, "But . . . this is hard. This isn't working. Some people don't like your ideas or you. Some people think your priorities are mixed up and that your intentions are wrong. Some people think your prices are too high. Some think they are too low. I don't feel like figuring it out. I don't know how. This is a lot of work."

My brain says these things to me all the time, but on a good day I answer it. I choose faith. I choose to believe in the future I am creating for myself, my family, and most of all, my clients. Then I answer my brain with, "We'll figure it out. Just keep going."

Ever have a friend spoil the end of a movie for you? When you watch a movie knowing how it's going to end, it's interesting when the story seems to be headed the opposite direction. You don't doubt that it will end the way you were told; you just wonder how. You stay engaged, wanting to see how the writers took the story from where it is now to where you know it's going to end up. You can do this with your own goals and stories too, you know. You can decide that even though things seem to be headed in the opposite direction, they will turn around. You don't even have to know how. You can just have faith.

Having faith is what we do as members of The Church of Jesus Christ of Latter-day Saints. We choose to believe that while life is challenging, fear is not necessary because we know that things will work out in the end. President Thomas S. Monson expressed this belief when he said, "We need not despair. . . . We are waging a war with sin. . . . It is a war we can and will win."[8] This faith in the Lord's plan gives us peace even when it feels like we are losing the war against sin, doubt, hopelessness, or other challenges we might face as we pursue our spiritual and temporal goals. We can apply the kind of faith President Monson described to any righteous desire.

As of today, more than ten thousand individuals have participated in the Be Bold coaching program and have applied the tools to their lives. They have taken the concepts they've learned and have improved themselves, their homes, and their communities. Every day people send me messages like this one:

Dear Jody,

I need to express my appreciation to you and the work you are doing. Thank you for helping others like me who can benefit and grow by applying these simple truths. I'm still in the learning process of this, but I want you to know I feel that I have finally found the tools I have been looking for after many years of therapy, EMDR sessions, self-help reading, and support groups. Nothing quite did it for me in my recovery from past abuse. While I know I was guided and have benefited from these resources, I was getting to the point of believing that I would forever remain the victim of a narcissist in this life and my purpose was to learn how to deal with it.

The model you share has changed the way I see my life now. I can only be a victim if I choose to think that I am. There is no power in this thought and it hasn't served me and has left me feeling defeated every time I came in contact with my ex. Changing how I choose to view myself, the way God sees me, and believing in these more powerful truths, has left no more room for thinking I could be a victim of anyone. My purpose is so much greater than this. I know deep down I've always known this, but it wasn't until I learned how to apply the model that I have been able to

bring these truths to the surface. So thank you! Keep doing what you are doing because it's inspiring and life-changing!
—Be Bold Member

All of the women (and more men every day) who are in the program or have participated in the past are creating a wave of change. Just as I envisioned they would. And now I'm working on new goals that interest or inspire me. They are baby ideas, so I keep them mostly to myself. I'm nurturing and loving them. I am not in a rush for them to grow up because there is no reason to hurry to the finish line. When you pursue a goal from faith, the finish line is no better than the experience of pursuing the goal. When, with faith, you choose to know without proof that you will succeed, you experience joy all along the way. I promise this is true, and not only for the goals we pursue; it's also true for the challenges we are working through.

You're allowed to believe that everything will turn out amazing at the end of your movie. You can decide that someone else already saw the movie and told you so because we know from the scriptures that this is the case. In John 16:33, Christ assures us that the movie ends well: "These things I have spoken unto you, that in me ye might have peace. In the world ye shall have tribulation: but be of good cheer; I have overcome the world."

Sometimes when you have big goals, your brain or other people will tell you that you're being unrealistic, but I believe that our world would not be the marvelous place it is today if people weren't willing to believe in unrealistic things. I'm so glad they did.

I believe that the Lord is guiding my life and that He has blessed me with everything I need to accomplish and create my righteous desires. I believe that through Him anything is possible. I believe that He wants me to rely on my knowledge and skills to accomplish my goals, and I believe that He wants me to continue to learn and then go and help others. I believe these and many other thoughts that some might say I have no business believing.

I choose to believe them anyway.

I choose faith.

Changing Your Lens Length

Having faith is essential as we work through both spiritual and temporal matters, such as achieving goals. But what about when life gets especially tough? What about when we experience trials or tragedies? How do we hold on to the faith that everything will work out and that there is nothing to fear when it appears that there is, indeed, something to fear and things are *not* working out?

As I write this, we are in the middle of the COVID-19 pandemic of 2020. People are buying toilet paper in bulk, and it feels as though life in general has been cancelled. These are uncertain times, and fear is a frequent visitor to many people. Even with the belief that the Lord is in charge, it's difficult to find your way to peace, faith, and love when Costco looks like the end of days and school is cancelled indefinitely. In times like this, I recommend that you shorten your lens.

Here's what I mean. Instead of worrying about what life will be like next year or next month or next week, let's just focus on today.

Our brains are masterful at problem solving. When we know the facts and parameters of a problem we are dealing with or a goal we are working toward, then we are incredibly resourceful, strategic, and creative. We find solutions and make things happen—or we take as much action as possible toward the result we want. This problem-solving action is energizing and feels useful. Although we may still experience overwhelm or stress, taking action feels less alarming to the brain than creating fear about a problem that we have no information about and therefore can't resolve yet. In other words, we can't solve a problem that might happen in the future but that isn't a current reality.

When my sister called and asked me to come to her boyfriend's house so she could tell me something, I knew it was serious. I could tell by the tone of her voice.

I was twenty-one years old at the time, and my two-years-younger sister Natalie and I had always been close. We were home from college for Thanksgiving break, and Natalie had been spending time with her high school boyfriend, whom she was still dating. As soon I got off the phone, I headed over to his house to see what was going on. I arrived to see Natalie waiting for me out front. With both hands pulled up under her winter coat to keep warm in the early Spokane winter, she sobbed and stared at her feet as she said, "Well, we had sex and now I'm pregnant." This unplanned pregnancy was a shock. But I was the big sister here. I was called in to help and had my big-sister superhero cape on, so my brain went to work sifting through this information to identify the problem. The following are the immediate "problems" I identified:

I had a sister who was emotional and needed comfort and assurance.

I had two parents at home who didn't know this news yet and would need to be looped in sooner than later.

I had a young couple in front of me who would have some decisions to make and could use some support and guidance.

So naturally, without realizing it at the time, I went to work "solving" these problems as best I could. "It's going to be OK,

Natalie," I told her as I gave her a hug. "We will figure this out. I will help you. I love you. Don't worry. We will get through this."

I kept talking to her, and as I did so, her emotions settled down a little bit. We started thinking about what to do, and my brain went to work on the next two problems. I recommended that she tell our parents. Our parents are not overreactors, so I knew they would handle the news as well as could be expected, and I knew that Natalie would feel a tremendous relief after that emotional conversation was behind her. She would also benefit from feeling their support and having guidance from them about what to do next.

I called my mom and dad to make sure they were both at home. I wanted to cushion the shock for them without telling them the news, so I simply said, "I'm coming over with Natalie and she needs to talk to you. It's important." I also gave Natalie some sisterly advice: "When you tell Mom and Dad you can leave off the part about you guys having sex. When you tell them you are pregnant they will figure that part out." She agreed.

Twenty-two years later, I can still feel the emotions of that day. I can still feel the cold that seemed to pierce the air and pierce our hearts. I feel the love I felt for my sister as I saw her pain. I feel the love I felt for that unborn baby who would end up being twin girls who blessed my sister's life when she reunited with them as young adults after placing them for adoption as babies. I can still feel the relief I felt when my parents reacted with pain and love in equal measure, as I knew they would. It was not an easy day. But each problem at hand that day was one I could begin to tackle. What was not solvable for any of us was the future.

A future problem leaves us waiting. We don't know what to do because we don't know what needs to be done. Sometimes there are precautionary measures we can take, but ultimately we can't do a whole lot of problem-solving without knowing what the challenges will be. A future problem is like a puzzle we want to put together but there are missing pieces and we don't have the box cover to show us the completed picture. It's impossible. The brain does not like this at all.

Enter worry.

Worry causes our minds to run wild with possible scenarios. In an attempt to latch on to something that it can solve, it creates stories about what could go wrong. But when we allow our brains to run away into the future and indulge in worry, we experience the opposite of faith. Faith says, "Whatever happens in the future, we will get through it." Worry says, "We're probably all going to die."

As Natalie's babies grew in her belly, I worried. I worried about her emotional health. She and the babies' father had broken up, and while I was secretly relieved, she was heartbroken. I worried about her spiritual health as I watched her go through a difficult repentance process. I worried about her future as she navigated decisions that seemed too important to get wrong but too unknown to know what was right. All of the future problems my brain came up with were much more painful than any problem happening in real time.

In real time, Natalie would sometimes feel nauseated, and I'd try to comfort her, make her whatever food sounded edible in the moment, and when all else failed, tell her it's OK to just stay in bed. In real time, we had to decide one day at a time whether she should stay in school or withdraw for a while. Whether she would go to class or skip it. That's it. Real time is doable. Even in our greatest challenges.

Shortening your lens length is a great way to minimize worry. Bring your mind back to the present moment. What is happening right now? Is there a problem we need to solve *right now?* Often the answer is, "No. Not really. Everything is fine right now." Or perhaps the answer is, "Yes. Breakfast. What am I going to eat for breakfast?"

Like Eckhart Tolle said, "Worry pretends to be useful but serves no useful purpose."[9] Worrying does not mean you are more well-informed or wise.

I promise you this.

I don't know what will be happening with the COVID-19 pandemic by the time you read this. I don't know what the end will be. I don't even know what the middle of the story will be. I don't know if things are going to get worse, and I don't know how long it will last. I don't know what challenges the pandemic will present for us globally, locally, or within my own home. Because I don't know any of these things, I can't take action to "fix" anything. I can prepare by having a few more groceries in my home than normal. I can do my best to keep our environment disinfected and remind everyone to wash their hands and wear a mask. I can pay attention to information coming from the school district, the CDC, and our Church leaders. Other than that, there is not really a problem to be solved, so I am going to keep my lens focused on one day at a time.

We need to figure out a plan for this semi-homeschool thing we're going to do now.

I need to figure out how to balance work with the kids.

That's about it. That's as far out as I can take my lens with regard to the pandemic right now. If I become infected with the virus, then there will be a different problem to solve. If my business doesn't survive it and we have no income, then I will focus on solving for that problem. If we are not allowed to leave our houses, again, that's a different problem. But, otherwise, I'm keeping my lens length in check. I only know what is happening right now, and the truth is, that's all we ever need to know.

One of my clients was a woman who was struggling because she had three young kids at home and her husband had recently passed away unexpectedly. She told me that she felt overwhelmed with all that lay ahead of her still. She wasn't sure how she was going to take care of her family and provide for them financially. She worried about whether her boys would struggle growing up with no man in the house and about her children not having their dad at their weddings. She couldn't imagine how she was going to handle living alone when her kids left the house one day. This was her model:

Circumstance: My husband passed away.

Thought: I don't know how I'll handle the rest of my life without him.

Feeling: Grief and overwhelm.

Action: Spin in overwhelm. Find more examples of situations in which it will be hard without him. Don't take action toward solutions. Don't know where to begin. Stay in bed as much as possible.

Result: I am not handling my life like I want to.

I told her that since she was in the midst of a huge change and grieving the death of her husband, we might want to shorten her lens. I suggested that instead of worrying about how her children were going to turn out and how she would find happiness as an empty nester (which wouldn't be happening for another fourteen years), we just focus on right here, right now. There was only one challenge she needed to tackle in the present, and it was big enough that she was going to need all hands on deck. It was grief.

Her main job right then was to allow pain for herself and figure out how to best support her children in their pain. Nothing else needed to be figured out at the moment, and thank goodness because this is enough for anyone.

As of the time we were working together, her finances were in order. She had enough money to live off of for many years. She had friends and family who were helping with things the kids needed help with. She had a home and food and everything else she really needed right then. I told her that this was the time to focus on her own self-care and to tell her brain that we don't need to solve for the future because we don't have any idea what it will be like when we get there. Here is her new model:

Circumstance: My husband passed away.
Thought: I need to focus only on emotional care for myself and my kids right now.
Feeling: Grief and peace.
Action: I find resources to help us grieve. I focus on one day at a time.
Result: We can do this.

Focusing only on current problems that are within our control is how we get to faith. The Lord will comfort us in hard times and help us through our challenges. But a challenge that hasn't even happened yet is different. Fear lives in the future. Faith says the future is unknown, but we are in the Lord's hands. There is nothing happening in the present moment that you can't handle with His help. As Christ said in John 8:12, "I am the light of the world: he that followeth me shall not walk in darkness, but shall have the light of life."

Shorter lenses are useful in many circumstances, but other times it's wise to lengthen your lens. I find this to be the case with goals or major changes we want to make. Bill Gates said that we overestimate the changes that could occur in the short term and underestimate potential changes over the long term,[10] and I notice this to be true for myself when I'm working toward changes in my own life.

I am carrying about twenty extra pounds on my body that I would love to let go of. I feel that I would be healthier, have more energy, and fit into my clothes better if I did. And the reason it's twenty pounds and not ten pounds is because my lens length was too short before.

Originally, I set out to lose ten pounds, and I wanted to do it quickly. I thought for sure that once I lost the weight I would feel better, be more confident, and life would be magical. So I did all the things you do when you're on a diet. I restricted my food and told myself to just deal with it when I was still hungry. I exercised significantly more and deprived myself of my usual forms of pleasure. This helped me lose ten pounds, and it felt great until soon thereafter the cravings, urges, and deprivation got the best of me and I began eating more to compensate for it. This overestimation of what I could or should be able to change in the short term was not loving me. It was the opposite. It was a disconnection from my body and myself, and it was an attempt to lose weight out of self-loathing. My model looked like this:

Circumstance: My body.
Thought: I need to lose ten pounds to be "good enough."
Feeling: Self-loathing.
Action: Deprive, overeat, repeat.
Result: Weight fluctuations and still not loving me.

Today I have lengthened my lens when it comes to my body and health. I decided that it might take me a year or two to lose these twenty pounds, and after a lot of work on my thoughts, I am OK with that because I know that changing my body size does not actually make me feel better or complete me. Only my thoughts can do that, which means I can choose to feel better today if I want to. But two years are going to go by, and I can be healthier or not by the end. Why not go for it? But I refuse to suffer or punish myself to get there. This longer lens means I don't have to.

Being committed for the long haul, observing my current patterns and relationship with food, and connecting with myself along the way are the actions I'm going to take to get to a place where I feel at my healthiest. I'm all in. There is no rush. This longer term perspective feels like love to me, and love is the only way I will allow myself to pursue weight loss now. My longer lens model looks like this:

> **Circumstance:** My body.
>
> **Thought:** I love this body and want to take care of it because I love it.
>
> **Feeling:** Connection.
>
> **Action:** Pay attention to my body, notice my patterns with curiosity, learn from myself, work on myself slowly.
>
> **Result:** I am connected with and loving me.

This lengthening of your lens, at its most effective, is having an eternal perspective. Viewing our lives and circumstances with an eternal perspective allows us to see them as they truly are. Elder Jay E. Jensen of the First Quorum of the Seventy said, "When we understand the great plan of happiness, we are gaining an eternal perspective, and the commandments, ordinances, covenants, and the experiences, trials, and tribulations can be seen in their true and eternal light. Remember, however, that Satan will dim the brightness of hope and eternal perspective by the dark, compelling urgency of now."[11]

When we think about ourselves and our lives as being eternal, we can see that there is nothing to fear. This life truly is a tiny moment in eternity. In the next life we will carry on, and because of the Atonement of Christ there is a safety net for the tightrope walk we are on right now. Falling is not a problem because Christ has already caught us. This thought brings me so much peace.

When my brain wants to worry about the economy, all the undone things on my to-do list, or my child struggling in middle school, I back up and remember that we are all eternal beings. The economy is seasonal, and it will always be. I will get done the things that really matter. And what's happening in seventh grade is not really going to matter eventually. I don't know how all of this turns out, but I know that the scriptures only say, "And it came to pass. . . ." They never say, "And it came to stay. . . ." Let's keep it in perspective, my friends—ideally an eternal one.

---

1. Articles of Faith 1:4.

2. Enos 1:7–8.

3. Ether 12:6.

4. 1 Nephi 17:8–9.

5. James 2:20.

6. Omar Itani, "10 Picasso Quotes That Will Inspire the Creative Artist in You," *Medium.com*, March 3, 2020, https://medium.com/swlh/10-picasso-quotes-that-will-inspire-the-creative-artist-in-you-1d4d0c0faa27.

7. Alma 56:48.

8. Thomas S. Monson, "Looking Back and Moving Forward," *Ensign*, May 2008, https://www.churchofjesuschrist.org/study/general-conference/2008/04/looking-back-and-moving-forward?lang=eng.

9. Eckhart Tolle, "Worry Pretends to Be Necessary but Serves No Useful Purpose," *The Quote Archive*, Tiny Buddha, accessed September 21, 2020, https://tinybuddha.com/wisdom-quotes/worry-pretends-necessary-serves-no-useful-purpose/.

10. Damon Brown, "This Perfect Bill Gates Quote Will Frame Your Next Decade of Success," *Inc.com*, https://www.inc.com/damon-brown/this-perfect-bill-gates-quote-will-frame-your-next-decade-of-success.html.

11. Jay E. Jensen, "Keep an Eternal Perspective," *Ensign*, April 2000, https://www.churchofjesuschrist.org/study/general-conference/2000/04/keep-an-eternal-perspective?lang=eng.

For we labor diligently to write, to persuade our children, and also our brethren, to believe in Christ, and to be reconciled to God; for we know that it is by grace that we are saved, after all we can do.

2 Nephi 25:23

14. EARTHLY LIFE

How do you feel about the word test? If you walked into a class and the teacher announced a test, how would you react? Would you be excited to examine your knowledge level, or would you, like most people, feel panic? Would you be thinking that now you have something to prove? That you're going to be told whether you are right or wrong and that it's much better to be right? Pressure's on.

The word *test* triggers several thoughts, and for most of us, they aren't peaceful or confidence-building thoughts. They are pressure-filled and frightening. But that's because we are thinking about the kind of tests that have an answer key, come with a consequence for too many wrong answers, and give you only one chance to prove your knowledge. But there are many different kinds of tests; for example, there are tests that simply provide useful information about our progress or knowledge gaps so that we know the best way to move forward, and we can take the test over again until we achieve a desired result.

I don't know about you, but as a young girl growing up in the Church, I felt all kinds of pressure and shame whenever I was taught that "life is a test." I was a mediocre student in school, and this "life test" sounded rather big and important. I was sure I could never measure up to it.

> **Circumstance:** Life.
> **Thought:** It's a test, and I'm not good at tests.
> **Feeling:** Defeated.
> **Action:** Get overwhelmed easily. Don't try as hard. Give up easily. Struggle to resist temptation. Seek false pleasure to feel better.
> **Result:** I'm not doing well at this life test.

I was also taught about the gift of the Atonement, but somehow I didn't completely understand its reality. Until I read Kim Giles's explanation that life is less like a test and more like a classroom,[1] I didn't fully grasp that, because of Christ's Atonement, life is not the kind of test that makes most people sweat. Yes, life is a test, but there are no grades; there are no right answers. There is only you exactly where you are in your spiritual progression and the experiences you will have that allow you to exercise your agency.

Elder David A. Bednar has also described the difference between the tests we take in school and the test we are taking during life. He said:

> Periodic tests absolutely are essential to learning. An effective test helps us to compare what we need to know with what we actually know about a specific subject; it also provides a standard against which we can evaluate our learning and development.
>
> Likewise, tests in the school of mortality are a vital element of our eternal progression. Interestingly, however, the word *test* is not found even one time in the scriptural text of the standard works in English. Rather, words such as *prove*, *examine*, and *try* are used to describe the various patterns of

demonstrating appropriately our spiritual knowledge about, understanding of, and devotion to our Heavenly Father's eternal plan of happiness and our capacity to seek for the blessings of the Savior's Atonement.[2]

I believe that in life, we are each given a personalized curriculum that is best suited to our own eternal progression. That curriculum is created in all sorts of ways. It might be through another person's agency, a natural disaster, a health diagnosis, a goal we choose to pursue, or our own decisions for good or for bad. Everything happening around us provides a curriculum that gives us opportunities to evolve and become more like God. Let's put it into a model:

Circumstance: Life.
Thought: It's a classroom, and I'm up for the learning.
Feeling: Curious.
Action: Seek to find the lessons. Keep striving to learn. Find my way back to compassion and love through repentance when I fall off track. Keep going.
Result: I'm progressing all the time.

I often wish I could choose my life classes—doesn't that sound great? In college I got to flip through a catalog and read course descriptions and then decide what my curriculum would be. In life, I have yet to receive my catalog, and I really didn't want to take some of these classes. I never signed up for my mother getting cancer. I didn't want depression and anxiety for several of my family members. None of us willingly enrolled in things like the Great Depression, the 9/11 attacks, or the COVID-19 pandemic. But wisdom would say that there is something bigger going on here and that suffering is part of the human experience and an important part of the plan. This doesn't mean that life isn't challenging or that we should always have a positive attitude. It means that it's helpful to remember that there is an eternal nature to our experiences. It means, essentially, that nothing has gone wrong.

Even when things have gone wrong.

Nothing has gone wrong.

Even when we willingly enroll in classes by choosing not to follow the commandments. This is the portion of our curriculum that we choose, but if we truly understand the Atonement and its gift of grace, then we know that nothing has gone wrong. This doesn't mean that we won't suffer or that some natural consequences won't be painful. We will, and they may. But Christ has already eliminated the grades. We only have to repent when we fall down. Repentance is the way to go back and correct our work and learn from it, and we get as many chances as we need to keep progressing. Remember, the Lord says in Mosiah 26:30, "Yea, and as often as my people repent will I forgive them their trespasses against me."

Trespasses against me is an interesting phrase. I don't think Jesus is talking about us offending Him or His honor—I think He is above being easily offended. Trespassing is about stepping over boundaries. If we cross someone's boundary, for example, by trying to control or otherwise mistreat this person, we can wound the individual and get in the way of him or her feeling Christ's love. We are called to be conduits of His love, not impediments to its flow. This concept applies equally to the way in which we treat ourselves. We can become quite good at erecting impediments to the flow of Christ's love in our own lives. But, fortunately, as often as we turn to Him, Christ will forgive us these trespasses and we can gain access to His love again. What an amazing gift.

So many of my clients who are righteous followers of Christ and who intend to follow Him are missing this understanding. They know about the power of the Atonement, but they don't always *know* it in reality. They worry when their kids make choices that are contrary to gospel teachings. They stress that they are not perfect enough themselves. They feel overwhelmed with all that we've been asked to do, and they feel inadequate.

I tell them that they have missed the point.

They've forgotten that life is a classroom.

They're forgetting that our kids' lives are classrooms, too. Our kids are not supposed to live free of challenges or mistakes. And neither are we. The Lord's plan was that we would be sent to earth, be told to keep the commandments, and mess it all up. That was *the plan*. That is not a mistake. That is not a disappointment. That is the way it was always going to go down. The plan is why we need the saving grace and strengthening power of Jesus Christ and His Atonement. We find this truth in Doctrine and Covenants 18:11: "For behold, the Lord your Redeemer suffered death in the flesh; wherefore he suffered the pain of all men, that all men might repent and come unto him."

As a young woman I was taught the law of chastity by loving, well-meaning individuals. I believe they wanted me to have the happiest life possible through obeying the commandments and minimizing the challenges that can come when we choose a different path. So they taught me about the commandment to reserve sexual intimacy for marriage (also known as the law of chastity), and they used some creative metaphors to get the point across. Perhaps you heard some of these metaphors when you were younger as well.

I clearly remember sitting in the chapel as a seventeen-year-old at a youth fireside and hearing the metaphor of the white cake. I was annoyed that I had to put on a dress and return to the church building on a Sunday evening, but I'd done so nonetheless, and now I was captive to the white cake story alongside my teenaged friends from the ward.

The Young Men president, who was our speaker, was prepared with a beautiful and delicious looking slice of white cake with white frosting. He explained that this piece of cake was like our bodies: white and pure and whole. Then he smashed that piece of cake right in front of our eyes and said that when we violate the law of chastity we become like this smooshed-up piece of white cake. No longer perfect, no longer whole, no longer pure. Just a big old sticky, crumbly mess. He drove the lesson home by reminding us that there is no way to put that piece of cake back together again. It was ruined forever.

First of all, I thought the cake still looked delicious because at age seventeen I didn't know much, but I knew that smashed cake still tastes delicious. I wondered if we were going to get to eat cake after the meeting. I assumed we would. That's what we do in Latter-day Saint culture. We eat cake.

But second of all, I felt committed to live the law of chastity. I really did. I felt the Spirit affirm that this is a good way to live. But there was a terror surrounding it as well. I felt the terror of knowing that I could end up like a smashed piece of cake and that I needed to be very careful or nobody could undo what I might do.

After hearing the white cake story, I committed to myself and to God to live a chaste life, and then I did my best to keep that commitment, so you might say that the Young Men president did his job well that night. In high school I had several boyfriends who were not members of the Church, and I was clear with them about my decision to remain chaste, which they respected when I put on the brakes if things got too heated.

But truthfully, I desperately loved being close to those boys. I loved kissing them and snuggling up to them. I even loved it when they desired me and I had to push them away. I loved being wanted by them, and then I felt ashamed for loving that. I believed that I loved something that was evil and worldly. I thought *I* was a little evil and worldly, and those seemed like disturbing things to be. So I tried to tuck that part of me away where nobody would see it. The only problem was, the hiding of it only seemed to intensify it.

Years later as a college student and then a young single adult, I continued to try to manage this part of me that loved boys and their affection but was committed to celibacy until marriage. It was exhausting being me. While I wasn't having sex, I was doing other things that the former Young Men president from my ward probably would have considered to be cake smashing. I knew I was crossing a line I had drawn for myself, and I felt a tremendous amount of guilt and shame and embarrassment over it.

I was failing the test.

Do you remember what we do when we are filled with shame and embarrassment? We hide. I hid from my Church leaders by making sure not to tell *anyone*. I hid from myself by disconnecting from myself, which is to say I talked to myself with criticism and self-loathing and avoided looking myself in the eye. I hid from God by not praying or reading my scriptures because I felt unworthy to do those things. I believed that I was not the perfect white cake I was supposed to be and that God was ashamed of me, and so I dug myself deeper and deeper into a ditch.

I didn't understand that the white cake metaphor was highly flawed. It didn't account for the most important part of the doctrine we believe in as members of The Church of Jesus Christ of Latter-day Saints. It excludes the part where Christ atoned for each of us, which means that the piece of white cake actually *can* be put right back together to its perfect, original state. The metaphor also doesn't account for the reality that we are not less loveable, beautiful, or amazing when we sin. We are still complete; we simply impede our spiritual health. I don't blame that Young Men president. He was doing the best he knew how, and I think the Lord teaches us line upon line, both as individuals and as a collective people. Today we know better. I'm pretty sure we've stopped using the cake metaphor to teach our youth. And I will forever be grateful for the bishop I had who understood the true power of the Atonement of Jesus Christ and explained it to me in the perfect way at the perfect time.

Bishop Lang is a Huntington Beach local who grew up surfing and has that laid-back surfer approach to life combined with a powerful testimony of Jesus Christ. His face is always tanned and his hair always a little sun bleached. He has laugh lines around his eyes from his lifelong exposure to the sun and the ever-present smile on his face. He is sort of famous—you might have heard of him. He's been a bishop I think thirty-seven times, and I do believe that if he wasn't so good at it, he wouldn't keep getting called. But through a divine act of grace, he was my bishop for a time.

In one of our singles ward sacrament meetings, the day after an activity where we had invited some recently married couples from our ward to return and participate in our version of the Newlywed Game, Bishop Lang stood at the pulpit and told us that Heavenly Father loved us and was mindful of our challenges and desires. Then he added, "Three of the four couples in last nights' Newlywed Game said that they kissed before even going on a first date, so I think we need a lot more kissing in this ward."

I decided that if I wanted to repent for the mistakes I felt I'd made Bishop Lang would be the one I could open up to, so I made an appointment to see him. Once again, I put on a dress and headed back to the church building on a Sunday evening, but this time I had a different experience. I felt the same spirit I'd felt years ago in that fireside, but this time there was no terror. There was only love. I cried and twisted my hands together as I told Bishop Lang about the things I'd done. I couldn't look him in the eye. I could hardly get the words out between sobs. But before long he interrupted me and asked me to give him the name of someone I am close to. Someone I love a lot.

I immediately thought of my sister Natalie, who was struggling after recently giving her twin baby girls up for adoption and trying to figure out where to go next in her life. I didn't tell him Natalie's story. I only gave him her name. Next he asked me what I would think about Natalie, and what I might say to Natalie if she were sitting in front of me, telling me the things I had just told him.

"I would tell her it's OK. Everything is going to be OK." As I said the words, I recalled that I had in fact said the same thing to her not all that long ago and in not all that different of a circumstance.

"Would you be mad at her or want her to stay away from you?" he asked me.

"No, of course not," I replied.

And then, that Sunday evening in Bishop Lang's office at church, I suddenly felt the hot shame leave my body and a warm love fill my heart instead. Not for me, but for my sister. I was filled with love and compassion, and I desperately missed her. I thought that if I could just show her how amazing and complete she is I would, but I also knew that she had to learn it on her own time and in her own way. And then Bishop Lang explained to me that the way I feel about my sister is only a tiny fraction of the way God feels about His children. He loves each of us more than we can comprehend. He loves us when we struggle and wants to connect with us even more during these times.

That's when everything changed for me. That's when I began to grasp, in some small way, the power of the Atonement. Which isn't to say I understand it all now, but only to say that I understand how completely incomprehensible and completely full of love and grace God's plan is.

Remember that when our Heavenly Parents sent us here to earth and told us to keep the commandments, They knew we were not always going to be able to do it. However, they knew that when we fell down, we would have the opportunity to connect with Them the most. Because sometimes when we fall down we become vulnerable enough to reach for Them.

Bruce Deel is the founder of City of Refuge, a nonprofit organization dedicated to helping and supporting individuals in the Atlanta area who are impacted by homelessness, drug addiction, prostitution, and other challenging circumstances.[3] In a recent podcast interview with Simon Sinek, Bruce shared a story about a gentleman he called Jake. Jake grew up in an extremely volatile and abusive home. He remembers hiding in the closet as a young boy with his siblings and mother as his father roamed the house in search of them with a gun. At a young age Jake left home to escape the trauma and eventually found himself homeless and addicted to drugs. Later in life, Jake met Bruce

Deel, who took him in. Bruce allowed Jake to live with him and his family. He loved him, and even though at times Jake would steal from him, lie to him, and violate his trust, Bruce decided there was no limit to the number of chances he would give Jake.

One day after he had been away for eight months, Jake once again made contact with Bruce, who said, "Come and stay with us for a while." Jake said that he couldn't—he couldn't be caged. But he did ask if he could just sleep in the back of Bruce's old Ford F150 truck. Bruce said of course he could, and Jake slept there many nights.

One morning a friend of Bruce's called him up to let him know that there was someone sleeping in his truck and he might want to check it out. Bruce replied that it was Jake, and his friend said, "No, it's not Jake. It's a larger gentleman." Bruce went to the truck to see who it was only to find that his beloved Jake had passed away in the night. His body had bloated in the truck and he no longer resembled his former self. He was gone.

As I listened to Bruce share this story, my heart hurt for these two men. And then I heard Bruce say this: "Jake came home to die. Maybe a part of him knew that he was close to the end of his life and he just wanted to be someplace where he felt safe and loved. He knew the back of my truck was his if he wanted it, and I'm glad he had a place to come home to at the end of his life."[4] Bruce, while not a member of the Church, is a religious man who has an eternal perspective that clearly gives him wisdom beyond what most of us can otherwise see.

We don't always get to choose our curriculum in this class-room of life. It's easy to notice the disproportionate amount of trials some are given relative to others. But then again, I'm always fascinated by people who choose to participate in a triathlon. Or enroll in an Ivy League school. Or do a five-thousand-piece puzzle.

Why would we purposely sign up for such things? Because we understand that taking on a challenge will require something of us. It will require that we stay connected to our highest selves. It will require self-discipline, commitment, and focus. In the process of meeting these expectations, we become a different version of ourselves, and then we get to appreciate our accomplishments at the end.

This is why God sent us to earth. He offered us a scholarship to earth school, and we jumped for joy. But now that we're here, we question its difficulty. I don't know why people like Jake have to take all the hardest classes while others seem to get only classes at the 101 level over and over again. So often we want it to be easier, or we believe something has gone wrong when trials come. But what if we're missing the point? What if these things are not happening *to* us but *for* us? What if we decided to use our challenges to access our highest selves? This is our opportunity. This is our classroom. This is His gift to us.

---

1. Kim Giles, "Life's Test Was Turned into a Classroom," *KSL.com*, December 21, 2015, https://www.ksl.com/article/37842526/lifes-test-was-turned-into-a-classroom.

2. David A. Bednar, "We Will Prove Them Herewith," *Ensign*, October 2020, https://www.churchofjesuschrist.org/study/general-conference/2020/10/12bednar?lang=eng.

3. City of Refuge (website), accessed September 22, 2020, https://cityofrefugeatl.org/.

4. Simon Sinek, "Second Chances with Bruce Deel," accessed September 22, 2020, episode 13, in *A Bit of Optimism*, produced by Simon Sinek, podcast, 25:17, https://simonsinek.com/discover/episode-13-second-chances-with-bruce-deel/.

For my thoughts are not your
thoughts, neither are your ways
my ways, saith the Lord. For as the
heavens are higher than the earth,
so are my ways higher than your ways,
and my thoughts than your thoughts.

Isaiah 55:8–9

15. GOD AND THE MODEL

Outside of the Model

The model is an amazing tool for helping us observe ourselves and the results we create in our lives. It gives us all of our power back by showing us that we are accountable for what we are thinking, experiencing, and ultimately creating. This concept is the opposite of what we were taught in the past by well-meaning people.

We were taught that other people can hurt our feelings.

We were told to be nice so we wouldn't hurt other people's feelings.

But what we were taught is backward, and it makes the world a scary place because it means that we have to navigate other people or try to control them, both of which are challenging, if you haven't noticed. The model puts the focus back on us. It tells us to be nice because being nice feels good and because we are nice people, rather than to be nice so that other people don't feel bad. It teaches us that we get to feel however we want to feel, no matter what anyone else says or does. It helps us decide what we want to do and who we want to be instead of trying to control the uncontrollable. It's an incredible relief to live this way.

Once upon a time, I had a talented hairstylist who was open to learning this model during the hours I sat in her chair so I could stay blonde. I taught her that other people are responsible for their own emotions and that when we stop trying to control others' feelings and instead focus on being who we want to be, we find peace. One day when I showed up for my appointment, my stylist was excited to tell me about her friend the accountant. She explained that this friend had wanted her to hire him but she didn't want to for various reasons. She said that before she learned what I had taught her, she would have been dishonest with him to avoid making him mad. She would have said yes and then later would have been angry at herself and resentful toward this man.

But she didn't do that this time.

She decided to love her friend and tell him "No, thank you," and then allow him to feel however he feels.

"I can't believe it," she told me. "I can't believe I never did this before."

"Do you think he's mad?" I asked her, and she said that he was for sure unhappy.

"But it's OK. I am just remembering what you told me, which is that I don't have to be mad at him for being mad at me. I respect him and admire him. I just need to tell the truth. I can't believe I waited so long to live this way. This is so much better."

I've found that it takes only one experience like this to feel how much more honest and empowered it is to live in control of yourself instead of trying to control others. I love getting to watch people put this concept into action and experience it for themselves.

Often, the question people ask me after they have such an experience is, "How does the Spirit fit in?" They want to know if the Spirit gives us thoughts or feelings. They ask me how they can tell if they are thinking their own thoughts or if their thoughts are coming from the Holy Ghost. They ask me where God fits in the model, and my answer is as follows.

The model is a tool for understanding *human* behavior. It's a useful way to become an observer of yourself, which gives you leverage over yourself. It helps you be more compassionate and understanding of others. But God does not operate as we do. His thoughts are not our thoughts, and His ways are not our ways.[1] We know that His experience and relationship with time is not something we can understand. He exists beyond the model.

So, does the Spirit give you a thought? A feeling? Does this mean that God can control our thoughts or feelings in some way? How does it all work? The truth is, of course, that I don't know. I couldn't possibly claim the ability to explain any of that, but I also think it's the wrong question to be asking. I don't think it matters whether He gives us thoughts or feelings or how God works in general. I think if our Heavenly Father thought it was necessary for us to understand this, He would tell us. I think that our need to have faith and trust without knowing is part of what completes our experience here on earth.

But here's what I do believe: I believe that God, Jesus Christ, and the Holy Ghost are perfect, loving beings. I believe that They love us completely and perfectly all of the time and that They want joy and growth and eternal life for us.

Imagine a large building with numerous rooms. God and Christ are in the room that is love and trust and faith. The room is filled with those emotions, and the door is wide open. Anyone is welcome inside. But if you are not feeling those same emotions, you won't feel comfortable in that room. God will invite us in, but it's up to us to choose to think about ourselves and our lives in such a way that we feel those same feelings and enter that room with Them.

When we feel fear and judgment and shame we are in a different room. That room is on the opposite side of the building from where God is. We have to navigate our way through the building using different emotions like compassion and curiosity, which lead to the feelings we want—the feelings that all three members of the Godhead live from.

I believe the question we should be asking ourselves is not, How does God influence us? but rather, How can I get to the place where He is and I can hear Him? Or in other words, How can I keep myself open to receive and recognize His influence?

And the answer to this question is to clean up our thinking.

The Power of Clean Thinking

Cleaning up my thinking is the continuous work of my life. It is the work I strive to do every day and the work I plan to continue to do until I die. Observing and choosing our thoughts is how, as humans, we are able to operate at the effect of our higher, wiser human brains rather than at the effect of our primal brains. But we will never finish this work in our lifetime. It is not a checkbox to mark off but rather a reoccurring task necessary to access the Spirit and live the kind of life that we create with the Spirit's guidance. Just as we will regularly make mistakes in this life and therefore will often need to repent, we will continually have thoughts that don't serve us and will frequently need to examine and clean up our thinking.

My home has beautiful, dark brown hardwood floors. I am grateful for this home and these floors, especially after many years of renting tiny houses in humble circumstances. I live with my family and our pets, so the floors get dirty quickly. House-work isn't my favorite thing, and motivating myself to mop the floor is a challenge I have yet to master. I usually put it off and have found that I can avoid it for a long time if I do one simple thing regularly.

Sweep.

The more often I sweep the floors, the less often I have to mop. I'm not sure why sweeping seems to be less of a burden. Perhaps it's easier to grab a broom than to get water involved and keep the kids and the pets from walking on the floor while it dries. At any rate, I sweep on the regular so I can avoid heavy-duty mopping as much as possible. In a similar way, I keep my thinking clean so my heart can live in love and trust and invite the Spirit into my life. Regularly doing the small things keeps my mind focused on useful thoughts so that I have less heavy-duty thought-work to do to be the person I want to be.

What are the small things? What is "sweeping" when it comes to thought-work?

Come on. You know this one.

You say these things out loud all the time. You give these answers in church every week. You tell yourself you *should* be doing these things, but you may be mistaken about the reasons for doing them:

Seeking answers in the scriptures.
Connecting with God through prayer.
Attending your Church meetings with an open mind and heart.
Remaining temple worthy and attending as time permits.
Spending quality time with family.
Serving others with a willing heart.

These activities "sweep" our brains. They keep us thinking clean. They help us keep our minds focused on an eternal perspective so that, no matter what happens in this life, we remember that it is only a tiny moment of eternity. They help us stay close and connected to our Heavenly Father so that we can remember our divine heritage and His perfect love for us. They help us have thoughts of gratitude and abundance for the goodness in our lives. They help us feel more love and compassion for ourselves and others. They keep us centered on Christ.

Having an eternal perspective, remembering our divine heritage, pondering God's love for us, being thankful for all we have, coming up with ways to love and serve others—this is thinking in its cleanest, purest form.

I journal regularly to find out what's happening in my brain. When I want to talk through things, I go to my coach, who can show me my brain from a completely objective place. I regularly listen to others get coached. I put my thoughts and problems into models, and I use the model to observe myself when I am facing a challenge or working on a goal. I do all of this work to keep myself from needing the heavy-duty mopping that is otherwise required when I let my brain and emotions run away from me.

Now, I want to be clear that there is nothing wrong with needing a good mop every now and then. At times in my life I have needed deep coaching, therapy, and guidance from a bishop. Sweeping is not a fix-all for the human condition. Sometimes we have biological factors such as hormone or chemical imbalances, and some people have experienced traumatic events that require regular mopping. There is no shame in any of this. But I know that if you choose to pay more attention to controlling your own thoughts and less to trying to change things outside of you, you will see tremendous progress in your mental and emotional health. I also know that the more often you do the little things we are taught to do (sweeping), the less often you will need more serious interventions (mopping).

My dear friend Bev Aron once told me that every year on their birthdays she used to read her children a book called *Before You Were Born*. It tells the story of the angel Lailah, who used to visit you in your mother's belly as you grew there. Lailah revealed to you the secrets of the universe, taught you the languages of the animals, and showed you all there was to know about the past and the future. Then, just before you were born, she pressed her finger to your lips and told you to keep all of this wisdom a secret. As she pressed her finger to your lips you magically forgot all of it, and her finger left a small indent in your upper lip. You can feel it now if you run your finger over it.[2]

Ever hear something and have the feeling that you already knew it, but you'd somehow forgotten? Maybe it's because you *did* know it once before. Perhaps you knew it in the premortal world. Perhaps it was taught to you by an angel at some time in some way. But somehow you recognize it as truth. I find tremendous beauty in the mystery of it all—the not knowing how it works but trusting that anything loving and good is of God.[3] And furthermore, trusting that the Spirit will reaffirm goodness if we ask.[4] Joseph Smith, who significantly understood the power of asking in faith, said, "One of the grand fundamental principles of 'Mormonism' is to receive truth, let it come from whence it may."[5]

Sometimes when I'm coaching or teaching I have small but powerful moments when it feels like wisdom is pouring out of me. Like it's not me talking at all—it's something much higher and wiser than me. The words are coming out of my mouth, but even as I'm saying them I am fascinated at what I'm hearing. It lasts for only a moment or two, and I don't usually let anyone in on the secret that I don't know where those words came from. I simply allow myself to be open to the wisdom, and I say it out loud, all the while thinking, *That was good. I should write that down.*

What is this experience?

Is it just my own head spouting nonsense? Maybe.

Is it God guiding me?

I don't know. It feels presumptuous of me to assume that God is guiding me like that. But it also feels dismissive to think that it couldn't be.

I don't know exactly what I'm experiencing in those moments, but I suspect that we all have moments like this. We all have times of clarity and wisdom and love, and on those occasions we are lining up with righteousness, with love, and with the Spirit. It is my hope that I can invite more of that wisdom into my life by sweeping my mind of fear and judgment and making room for the mysteries of God.

---

1. Isaiah 55:8–9.

2. Howard Schwarz, *Before You Were Born* (New York: Roaring Brook Press, 2005).

3. Moroni 7:12–13.

4. James 1:5.

5. Joseph Smith, quoted in *History of the Church of Jesus Christ of Latter-day Saints*, 2nd ed. (Salt Lake City: Deseret News Press, 1949), 5:499.

Adam fell that men might be;
and men are, that they
might have joy.

2 Nephi 2:25

16. BETTER THAN HAPPY

What Could Be Better?

Just over a year ago, my husband and I took our kids to Disneyland. They say it's the happiest place on earth, and I think they might be right. It was our kids' first time there because in the past we were unwilling to spend the money and time to go since our kids were afraid of rides, were impatient with lines and crowds, and said they didn't really care to go. But when a family in our ward invited us to join them on a trip there, we decided it was time that our kids learned what they were missing out on.

Disneyland is truly a magical place. It is full of people yet spotlessly clean. Even the trash cans are clean and well-placed.[1] Magical. The only problem you need to solve the entire time you are there is deciding which ride you want to use your next fast-pass on and whether you should have a churro now or later or both. My kids loved Disneyland more than I thought they would. They warmed up to the rides, and everyone was so happy so much of the time I wondered if there was something questionable being pumped out of those gutters there on Main Street.

I love the many experiences available to us in this life, such as Disneyland, that allow us to feel happy an inordinate amount of time. It is human nature to seek them. We believe that happiness is the best thing. It motivates us more than anything else. We seek things that we believe will allow us to feel happiness (even though happiness is always created by our thoughts), such as a romantic relationship, a new house, more money, a slimmer body, a nice vacation, the completion of our to-do list, and approval from others. It's OK that we do this. As long as we are keeping our desires aligned with our values, it's not a problem to seek happiness from outside things. But it becomes a problem when we start chasing something that we can never truly catch or when we do so at the expense of what matters most. Like my cat, who can't really catch the light from a laser pointer, we can't catch happiness the way we believe we can. Happiness is fun, but it is fleeting. It is temporary. It's an itch that never truly gets scratched, and it is not what we are designed for.

We are designed for something even better than happiness.

We are designed for joy, which is much more complex than happiness.

We crave growth and expansion.

We want and need the dynamic contrast that life provides.

Feeling alive is more fulfilling than feeling happy.

Perhaps this is semantics, and perhaps happiness and joy and expansive living are not all that different from one another, but I think there is more to it than semantics. I believe that what we crave is much deeper and longer-lasting than we know. It's the feeling of accessing your highest, most loving, most trusting, most Christlike self. It's a feeling that comes and goes, but unlike simple happiness, truly feeling alive changes us because it requires that we overcome something or be more intentional with our thoughts, feelings, and actions. And the better you get at conscious thinking, the more full and rewarding your life becomes.

Even happiness requires a contrast of emotions. Without pain we can't feel joy. Without suffering we can't feel relief. Without fear we can't feel trust. Without contempt we can't feel love. Yes, we came here to earth to experience joy, but we had to enter this mortal state to experience it because mortality is what allows for the full experience of being alive. I find it interesting that in this well-known verse of scripture the Fall of Adam and our ability to feel joy are discussed together: "Adam fell that men might be; and men are that they might have joy."[2]

Perhaps the Fall, which is the reason we make mistakes, judge others, lack faith, or create problems for ourselves, is the necessary contrast to joy. The Fall brought contrast. Opposition in all things. Something to push back against. This is how we get to joy. Joy is better than happiness. Happiness is lovely, but it's also sort of boring.

Joy requires presence. It requires that you be here now. Happiness is "I can't wait to go on vacation—it's going to be so fun," referring to the future, and "Remember how nice it was when the kids were younger and they didn't talk back like they do now?" in reference to the past. But joy is not about antici-pating a future moment or recalling a past memory. Joy lives in the right here, right now. Happiness is riding a roller-coaster at Disneyland. Joy is watching my child's face when he realizes he rode it even though he was terrified to do so. Joy changes him by giving him a bit more confidence than he had before, and it changes me by creating a memory and bond with my child.

Happiness exists in moments when things are going how we thought they should go, but joy exists even in the midst of chaos. Joy is the peaceful reassurance that somehow everything will be OK, even if OK is not what you pictured, as you sit in a hospital waiting room awaiting news. It exists in the embrace of your child. It exists in the comforting wisdom of your husband. It exists in the small moments that you never could have predicted and rarely can fabricate.

Happiness says, "What should we do next?"

Joy says, "Everything we need is right here in this moment."

Happiness is planning an outing for your family to go on together at a special time.

Joy is soaking in the sound of everyone helping clean up after dinner on an ordinary Tuesday.

Happiness requires something outside of the norm.

Joy is seeing the magic in the mundane.

Happiness can't wait to achieve a goal.

Joy knows that the process of getting there is the best part.

Happiness hopes that one day the house will stay clean for a bit longer.

Joy recognizes that truly living is messy.

Happiness loves a compliment from another person.

Joy knows the compliment tells us more about the person giving it than the one receiving it.

Happiness comes from the thought that, finally, things are complete for a moment.

Joy comes from the thought that nothing was ever missing in the first place.

When I first discovered the tools of conscious thinking I worried that they were not acceptable in Latter-day Saint culture. The most famous life coach I knew of was Martha Beck, and she had been raised a member of the Church but later left. I was afraid that if I followed these tools they would lead me down a similar path or I would somehow disappoint my family and friends who were faithful members. But my experience has been the exact opposite of that. My testimony of the gospel of Jesus Christ has been strengthened as I've learned that I have the ability to choose my thoughts and that the thoughts I think will play out in my life in powerful ways. Christ is the perfect example of clean thinking. When He lived here on earth, He showed us what it looks like. In Matthew 8 we read about Christ and His disciples on a stormy sea. His disciples were afraid and couldn't understand how He could be sleeping, but He demonstrated that because of His great faith (His thought that there is nothing to fear and that through God anything is possible), He could create the miraculous result of calming the sea.[3] Perhaps His model looked something like this:

> **Circumstance:** Stormy sea.
> **Thought:** We need not fear.
> **Feeling:** Faith.
> **Action:** Remind disciples of the power of faith in word and in action. Calm the sea.
> **Result:** There is nothing to fear.

We don't have to achieve the level of mastery over ourselves that Christ demonstrated in order to feel the benefits of choosing our thoughts. And choosing our thoughts doesn't look like being happy all the time. Christ experienced all emotions. I know I will never be as good at clean thinking as Christ is, but along with His example He gave us the Atonement, which makes up for our shortcomings. There is literally nothing to fear.

Recently I was driving to pick my daughter up from preschool and was running late. I nervously tapped my hand on the door handle as I waited for the light to turn green, and when it did and the car in front of me didn't go right away, I felt a surge of frustration rise within me. I had thoughts like, *Come on, buddy! Pay attention! Move it!* Just before the gentleman stepped on the gas I noticed a sticker on his back window that read "Vietnam Veteran." Upon reading that my emotions shifted to compassion. I thought, *Oh, he's a Vietnam veteran. I'm so grateful to him and I wonder what his life has been like. He also must be older, and I wonder if he is healthy? This is OK. He doesn't need to hurry for me.* As I continued down the road toward my destination I recalled a similar experience in which I had been on the receiving end of someone's impatience.

Years ago, when I was overdue to deliver one of my babies, I was at the grocery store late at night picking up a few things. As I stopped to load something into my cart, a gentleman behind me asked me in an irritated voice to move over so he could get by. When I turned around to see him, he noticed my huge pregnant belly, and his demeanor immediately changed.

"I'm so sorry. I didn't realize you were in a delicate condition," he said. I remember this experience clearly because he called pregnancy a delicate condition and I thought that was an interesting way to describe it.

In my car that day on the way to pick up my daughter, I thought about how we do this to people. We judge them and we are irritated with them and their shortcomings, but sometimes, when we catch a glimpse of their challenges we soften. We lose judgment and move into compassion as our thoughts about this other person change. But what if we just assumed that everyone is in a delicate condition? Because we all are, aren't we? It's called the human condition. And even though we don't always wear it on our bellies or sticker the back of our cars with it, we all have places inside of us that are delicate. Terribly delicate.

Those places are worthy of compassion and love. Not judgment and hate. Learning to see others in this way is again what Christ shows us how to do and what we can strive for if we choose. This is better than happiness. This is love.

Next to my knowledge of the gospel of Jesus Christ, understanding the power of my thoughts in creating my experiences has changed my life more than anything else. In other words: "If you feel stuck in your present life, if you feel no enthusiasm for anything, if you think you have no purpose or that you lost that purpose somewhere along the way, I guarantee you are living in a dungeon made of stories. And that none of those limiting stories are true."[4]

I definitely want to embrace the entire experience of being alive. I'm not always good at it. I still chase happiness, and in the process I distract myself from truly living. I make more mistakes than I could possibly count. I feel all of the emotions that humans experience, and some of these emotions are useful, while many of them are not.

But I am striving to embrace the complete experience of both pain and peace, which I call joy.

I know I was meant for joy, and I know it's available to me when I stop trying to control the things outside of me and then get still and deliberate with my thoughts and feelings.

Do you know what's better than simply being happy?

Attempting to understand and embrace your unfathomable worth.

Recognizing the completeness of everyone around you.

Being willing to fail in the name of showing up in your life.

Trusting that everything in this life is orchestrated in favor of your progression.

Learning to become good at something that first requires you to be very bad at it.

Continuously evolving your personal experience of God.

Loving people who don't even like you.

Staying open enough to constantly be learning.

Loving yourself no matter what.

Taking full accountability for every result you experience and having compassion with yourself.

In other words, what's better than happy is this moment.

Right here.

Right now.

---

1. "The Beauty of the Trash Cans of Disney World," Mickey Blog, January 10, 2019, https://mickeyblog.com/2019/01/10/beauty-trash-cans-disney-world/.

2. 2 Nephi 2:25.

3. Matthew 8:23–27.

4. Beck, Martha. *Steering by Starlight: The Science and Magic of Finding Your Destiny* (New York: Rodale, 2009), 53.